DISORDERS
FIRST
DIAGNOSED
IN CHILDHOOD

THE ENCYCLOPEDIA OF PSYCHOLOGICAL DISORDERS

Senior Consulting Editor Carol C. Nadelson, M.D.
Consulting Editor Claire E. Reinburg

DISORDERS FIRST DIAGNOSED IN CHILDHOOD

Daniel Partner

CHELSEA HOUSE PUBLISHERS
Philadelphia

The ENCYCLOPEDIA OF PSYCHOLOGICAL DISORDERS provides up-to-date information on the history of, causes and effects of, and treatment and therapies for problems affecting the human mind. The titles in this series are not intended to take the place of the professional advice of a psychiatrist or mental health care professional.

Chelsea House Publishers
Editor in Chief: Stephen Reginald
Production Manager: Pamela Loos
Art Director: Sara Davis
Director of Photography: Judy L. Hasday
Managing Editor: James D. Gallagher
Senior Production Editor: J. Christopher Higgins

Staff for DISORDERS FIRST DIAGNOSED IN CHILDHOOD
Prepared by P. M. Gordon Associates, Philadelphia
Picture Researcher: Gillian Speeth, Picture This
Associate Art Director: Takeshi Takahashi
Cover Designer: Emiliano Begnardi

The Chelsea House World Wide Web address is
http://www.chelseahouse.com

First Printing

9 8 7 6 5 4 3 2 1

Library of Congress Cataloging-in-Publication Data

Partner, Daniel.

Disorders first diagnosed in childhood / by Daniel Partner.
  p.   cm. — (The encyclopedia of psychological disorders)
Includes bibliographical references and index.
Summary: Examines the symptoms, causes, and treatment of disorders that appear in childhood, including autism, tic disorders, and pervasive development disorders.
ISBN 0-7910-5312-1
1. Preschool children—Mental health—Juvenile Literature. 2. Affective disorders in children—Diagnosis—Juvenile literature. 3. Behavior disorders in children—Diagnosis—Juvenile literature. 4. Mental illness—Diagnosis—Juvenile literature. [1. Mental illness.] I. Title. II. Series.
RJ499.P36   1999
618.92'89—dc21   99-30847
                                                                         CIP

CONTENTS

PSYCHOLOGICAL DISORDERS AND THEIR EFFECT

CAROL C. NADELSON, M.D.
PRESIDENT AND CHIEF EXECUTIVE OFFICER,
The American Psychiatric Press

There are a wide range of problems that are considered psychological disorders, including mental and emotional disorders, problems related to alcohol and drug abuse, and some diseases that cause both emotional and physical symptoms. Psychological disorders often begin in early childhood, but during adolescence we see a sharp increase in the number of people affected by these disorders. It has been estimated that about 20 percent of the U.S. population will have some form of mental disorder sometime during their lifetime. Some psychological disorders appear following severe stress or trauma. Others appear to occur more often in some families and may have a genetic or inherited component. Still other disorders do not seem to be connected to any cause we can yet identify. There has been a great deal of attention paid to learning about the causes and treatments of these disorders, and exciting new research has taught us a great deal in the past few decades.

The fact that many new and successful treatments are available makes it especially important that we reject old prejudices and outmoded ideas that consider mental disorders to be untreatable. If psychological problems are identified early, it is possible to prevent serious consequences. We should not keep these problems hidden or feel shame that we or a member of our family has a mental disorder. Some people believe that something they said or did caused a mental disorder. Some people think that these disorders are "only in your head" so that you could "snap out of it" if you made the effort. This type of thinking implies that a treatment is a matter of willpower or motivation. It is a terrible burden for someone who is suffering to be blamed for his or her misery, and often people with psychological disorders are not treated compassionately. We hope that the information in this book will teach you about various mental illnesses.

The problems covered in the volumes in the ENCYCLOPEDIA OF PSYCHOLOGICAL DISORDERS were selected because they are of particular importance to young adults, because they affect them directly or because they affect family and friends. There are individual volumes on reading disorders, attention deficit and disruptive behavior disorders, and dementia—all of these are related to our abilities to learn and integrate information from the world around us. There are books on drug abuse that provide useful information about the effects of these drugs and treatments that are available for those individuals who have drug problems. Some of the books concentrate on one of the most common mental disorders, depression. Others deal with eating disorders, which are dangerous illnesses that affect a large number of young adults, especially women.

Most of the public attention paid to these disorders arises from a particular incident involving a celebrity that awakens us to our own vulnerability to psychological problems. These incidents of celebrities or public figures revealing their own psychological problems can also enable us to think about what we can do to prevent and treat these types of problems.

Ideally, childhood is a happy time free of emotional or psychological problems. Unfortunately, the reality is not always so pleasant; psychologists have identified 10 categories of disorders that are usually diagnosed in childhood or adolescence—some even in infancy.

DISORDERS FIRST DIAGNOSED IN CHILD-HOOD: AN OVERVIEW

We may think of childhood as a period during which we are virtually immune to psychological problems. After all, our boyhood and girlhood years are supposed to be a simpler, less stressful time of life. The fact is, however, that many psychological disorders have their roots in childhood.

The fourth edition of the American Psychiatric Association's *Diagnostic and Statistical Manual of Mental Disorders (DSM-IV)* lists 10 categories of disorders that are typically first diagnosed during infancy, childhood, or adolescence. Some children who are diagnosed with these disorders will outgrow them. In many cases, however, the conditions will endure throughout life.

There are numerous different causes for these problems, including genetics and environment. A number of the disorders seem to stem from a malfunction of the chemicals that carry messages from one brain cell to another. Others have their roots in different neurological abnormalities. In most cases, biological causes combine with factors in a child's environment to produce the particular behaviors typical of each disorder.

This volume of the ENCYCLOPEDIA OF PSYCHOLOGICAL DISORDERS presents each of the *DSM-IV* categories of disorders first diagnosed in childhood. Based on the latest research, the discussion includes actual cases that allow the reader to become familiar with real-life examples of children and their families who face these problems.

Clearly, correct treatment of these disorders depends on correct diagnosis. Once health care providers have identified a child's particular problem, the youngster can get the help that he or she needs. Although many of the conditions are lifelong, treatment can alleviate symptoms and offer hope to the children and to the families of the children who confront these disorders.

Family love is an important factor in a person's emotional development, but many psychological disorders have a biological component. Children can develop problems no matter how warm and stable their home environments are.

INTRODUCTION

We like to think of childhood as a warm, happy, carefree time of life. Many individuals actually experience these idyllic circumstances, but for others childhood is not so easy. Some children, adolescents, and even babies must confront the onset of psychological problems.

The *DSM-IV* lists 10 categories of disorders that are typically first diagnosed during infancy, childhood, or adolescence:

1. mental retardation
2. learning disorders
3. motor skills disorder
4. communication disorders
5. pervasive developmental disorders
6. attention-deficit and disruptive behavior disorders
7. tic disorders
8. feeding and eating disorders of infancy or early childhood
9. elimination disorders
10. other disorders of infancy, childhood, or adolescence (including separation anxiety disorder, selective mutism, reactive attachment disorder, and stereotypic movement disorder)

Childhood can be a vulnerable period in an individual's development. During this time, genetics and environment lay the groundwork for adult personality. With the knowledge that the psychological disorders of children are frequently the precursors of adult problems, health care providers pay considerable attention to these serious—but often treatable—conditions.

Like this little girl, most children experience intense separation anxiety at one time or another. They may also wet their beds or become defiant for brief periods. Mental health professionals must therefore take great pains to distinguish a true psychological disorder from a normal stage of a child's development.

The *DSM-IV* describes these childhood disorders as unique and separate entities. In fact, however, many of the conditions appear in combination with one another. The *American Psychiatric Press Textbook of Psychiatry* states that "multiple psychiatric disorders are typical in a single child psychiatric patient." When the original disorder leads to secondary complications, intertwining and expanding behaviors can make it difficult for health care providers to sort problems into neat, separate categories.

As children develop, their various disorders may interact with one another in different ways. A toddler who is diagnosed with a communication disorder, for example, may as a school-aged youngster be found to have attention-deficit disorder and may later be diagnosed as suffering from intermittent explosive disorder (a problem in which a person has uncontrollable outbursts of temper) in adulthood. The outcome for each individual child will vary; this typically depends on heredity, environment, and treatment.

Because children change and develop as they grow older, the disorders that affect them will differ. For this reason, evidence of one of these conditions in a child or adolescent does not necessarily indicate that specific behaviors and limitations should be expected. Children with psychological disabilities grow and learn as all children do. Even in cases where a cure is unlikely, children and their families can learn new ways to cope with their conditions.

Even normal childhood development can cloud the diagnosis of these disorders. For example, most toddlers go through a period of intense separation anxiety, all children wet the bed at one time or another, and most two-year-olds and adolescents experience periods of defiant behavior. In addition, "normal" development varies from child to child. In *The Treatment of Psychiatric Disorders*, William H. Reid, George U. Balis, and Beverly J. Sutton state, "The developmental level of the child

Developmental disorders can lead to family stress of the kind shown here. Parents may try to find someone to blame for such problems—either themselves or their child.

has a major impact on how a disorder will be expressed and what treatments will be effective. Some behaviors are part of normal development at one age and evidence of disorder at another age." Dr. Jerrold S. Maxmen and Dr. Nicholas G. Ward concur, writing in *Essential Psychopathology and Its Treatment* that all too often "normal behavior may become confused with psychopathology." For this reason, careful professional evaluation is essential to accurate diagnosis.

THE DIAGNOSTIC PROCESS

The first people to notice that a child is having problems are usually the youngster's parents. For example, when an infant is slow to achieve developmental milestones, such as smiling, rolling over, standing, talking, and walking, the mother and father are likely to be aware of the delay before anyone else. Whether or not such variations indicate a disorder, however, is a question that can be answered only with the help of health care specialists.

Sometimes problems may not become apparent until a child attends school. Within the learning environment, parents or teachers may become aware of one or more of the following behaviors:

- extreme worry or anxiety about attending school
- fidgeting—constant movement beyond normal play behavior
- frequent temper tantrums
- poor academic achievement despite great effort
- repeated disobedience and/or aggression

Most childhood disorders will be diagnosed early in a youngster's life, but occasionally a particular condition may not surface until later in childhood. Preadolescents or adolescents will sometimes show the same symptoms as younger, school-aged children. In addition, however, they may exhibit one or more of the following behaviors:

- aggressive or nonaggressive violation of the rights of others
- alcohol and/or drug abuse
- depression (prolonged negative moods, often accompanied by poor appetite, difficulty sleeping, and/or recurrent thoughts of death)
- frequent outbursts of rage

DEVELOPMENTAL MILESTONES (AVERAGE AGE FOR HEALTHY INFANTS)

Although the following milestones are typical for the ages given, all children progress through these stages at their own rates. Significant failure to meet several of these milestones at the appropriate age, however, may indicate that a child needs diagnostic evaluation for a psychological or developmental disorder.

AGE	BEHAVIOR
1 month	sucks, grasps
3 months	smiles
5 months	sits up
6–8 months	crawls
8 months	experiences stranger anxiety
9 months	experiences separation anxiety
11 months	walks
15 months	imitates vocal sounds
18 months	talks (a few words)
22 months	uses toilet

- inability to cope with problems and daily activities
- opposition to authority
- truancy, theft, and/or vandalism

Again, diagnosis can be difficult, since many adolescents who do not have a psychological disorder experience some of these same symptoms. Parents who observe that their child's undesirable behaviors are more frequent than or more extreme than those of other children in the same age group should seek medical advice.

A comprehensive evaluation will help determine if a psychological disorder applies. The diagnostic analysis may involve input from a variety of professionals, including pediatricians, school psychologists, speech and language therapists, occupational and physical therapists, social workers, neurologists, and psychiatrists.

Early diagnosis is important for effective treatment to take place. Recall that various disorders may overlap. As the child grows, and as one condition influences another, the problems can expand to affect more

WHAT IS A COMPREHENSIVE PSYCHOLOGICAL EVALUATION?

To diagnose a child or adolescent with serious emotional and behavioral problems, a health care professional performs a comprehensive psychological evaluation. This can take several hours and more than one office visit. It may include parents and other family members as well as the child. The family physician, school personnel, and family members often provide information that assists in the evaluation, which may investigate any of the following factors:

- development
- family history of physical and psychological health, illness, and treatments
- family relationships
- present medical problems and symptoms
- school and social behavior

The diagnosis is generally also based on results from the following:

- laboratory studies (such as blood tests and X rays)
- psychological and educational evaluations (such as intelligence quotient [IQ] tests)
- psychological interviews and testing
- speech and language evaluations

Health care professionals use the information gathered to understand the child's problems and develop a treatment plan.

and more of the young person's life. Early intervention can prevent or halt this expansion of symptoms and increase the probability of successful treatment.

TREATMENT AND EDUCATION

The treatment of childhood disorders requires that the individual as well as the family and educational environments be addressed. Therapy must take into consideration the person's social identity. Because children are so dependent on their parents and other adults for their survival and for their quality of life, it is especially important to consider the role that children's social environment plays in their psychological well-being. For this reason, successful treatment typically combines family therapy and education with the child's individual treatment plan.

Since 1973, a series of federal and state laws and court decisions have supported the rights of individuals with disabilities to participate fully in all aspects of our society. Section 504 of the Rehabilitation Act of 1973, a civil rights law, prohibits discrimination against individuals with disabilities and provides for legal recourse in cases where discrimination may have occurred. The Americans with Disabilities Act, signed by President George Bush in 1990, strengthened the course set by Section 504. It is the intent of these laws to provide equal access—"reasonable accommodations"—to such facilities as transportation, telecommunications, education, and employment.

In 1975, the 94th Congress passed the landmark Education for the Handicapped Act, widely known as Public Law 94-142. Recently reauthorized as the Individuals with Disabilities Education Act (IDEA), this law provides states with federal funds to serve the needs of individuals with disabilities between the ages of 3 and 21. With the passage of IDEA, all preschool and school-aged students, regardless of the severity of their disability, must be provided an "appropriate education" in the "least restrictive environment." The process defined within this law requires that a multidisciplinary team, including the child's parent, conduct an evaluation to identify the student's eligibility and needs. The team then creates an individualized education plan (IEP) to devise a program appropriate for the individual child. To ensure that the educational program meets the child's current and evolving needs, it must be reviewed at least annually, with periodic reevaluations conducted at least every three years.

Before these landmark laws, children with disabilities, including psy-

This autistic girl is taking the field with her junior high school softball team. The Americans with Disabilities Act of 1990 prohibited discrimination on the basis of disability in employment, programs, or services offered by state and local governments; a federal judge ruled that under the law, the girl must be allowed to play.

chological disorders, were not guaranteed the right to an appropriate education. They were sometimes institutionalized and often excluded from the rest of society. Society was apt to view these individuals with suspicion, condemning them (or their parents) for their problems.

QUESTIONS THAT PARENTS OF CHILDREN WITH PSYCHOLOGICAL DISORDERS FREQUENTLY ASK

It is important for parents as well as the entire family (including the child) to understand the disorders in question. It is essential that they feel free to ask professionals for explanations and definitions if they are unsure about the meanings of words, terms, or any aspect of the disorder or the procedure for diagnosis and treatment. Some common questions include:

- Am I to blame?
- Can you help me?
- Can you help my child?
- Does my child need a special educational program?
- Does my child need more discipline?
- Does my child need treatment?
- Do I need treatment?
- How can the family help?
- How long will treatment take?
- Is there something wrong with my child?
- What are the long-range expectations for my child?
- What are your recommendations?
- What can the local public school do for my child?
- What will treatment cost?
- Will my child be able to measure up to other children?

We can still hear the echoes of such views today. But with the continuing application of science and technology, we continue to refine our understanding and treatment of childhood disorders. As our understanding of these conditions increases, so does our tolerance for the differences that are associated with them.

Because of her age, this woman may be at risk of giving birth to a baby with Down syndrome. Although the majority of children with this disorder are born to women under 35, the odds of a woman giving birth to a Down syndrome child increase when she passes 40.

2

MENTAL RETARDATION

When Janice Smith was 47, she became pregnant for the fourth time. This was not a planned pregnancy, but she and her husband were prepared to welcome the new addition to their family. When the baby was born, Janice immediately noticed that he looked different from her other babies at birth. His head was rounder, his face rather flat, his hands and ears very small. Janice and her husband named the baby Matthew.

The day after Matthew's birth, the doctor told the Smiths that the baby was a Down syndrome child (the term *syndrome* refers to a group of symptoms that occur together in a recurring pattern). The doctor explained that this meant that Matthew would be mentally retarded. The exact degree of *mental retardation* could not be determined until Matthew was older.

At first, Janice and her husband mourned for the "normal" baby that they had anticipated. They were not sure what to expect now. Would Matthew learn to walk and talk? Would he ever be able to care for himself independently? Would they be responsible for him the rest of their lives? How could they ever afford to retire if they had to support Matthew for his whole life?

As Matthew grew, however, his parents put aside some of their concerns. Matthew was an affectionate child with a ready smile, and the family could not imagine life without him. Still, Janice often felt exhausted by the level of care that Matthew needed. He was three and a half years old before he learned to talk and express his needs, and he was nearly five before he became toilet trained. Janice noticed that Matthew reached the same milestones that her other children had, but it took him much longer to do so.

Today, as Janice and her husband grow older, they worry about what will become of Matthew when they are gone. Will he ever be able to live independently? Will one of Matthew's siblings take over his care at some point? Or will they eventually be forced to consider residential care for him? Despite these concerns, despite all the challenges that they have faced caring for a mentally retarded family member, Janice is certain of one thing: Matthew has enriched their lives beyond measure.

According to the *American Psychiatric Press Textbook of Psychiatry*, roughly 1 to 3 percent of all people in the United States have some degree of mental retardation. Unfortunately, within the general population, misconceptions about mental retardation abound. Many people think of children like Matthew as "funny-looking," "weird," or "abnormal." And a mentally retarded adult is often considered to be still a child.

In fact, however—as Siegfried M. Pueschel, James C. Bernier, and Leslie E. Weidenman point out in *The Special Child*—a young child diagnosed as mentally retarded will not always be a child. Like any

Retarded children do not stay children forever. They grow up and face the same responsibilities as other adults, including the need to earn a living. Vocational education programs like the one shown here help the mentally retarded make the transition from dependence to employment.

youngster, the mentally retarded child will continue to learn, change, and grow intellectually—he or she will simply do so at a much slower rate.

WHAT IS MENTAL RETARDATION?

The *DSM-IV* lists three criteria for a diagnosis of mental retardation:

1. significantly subaverage intellectual functioning

2. significant limitations in at least two of the following skills:
   - communication
   - functional academic skills
   - health
   - home living
   - leisure
   - safety
   - self-care
   - self-direction
   - social/interpersonal skills
   - use of community resources
   - work

3. onset before 18 years of age

Similarly, the American Association on Mental Retardation defines this condition as "significantly subaverage intellectual functioning existing concurrently with related limitations in . . . adaptive skill areas" and manifested before age 18. The phrase "subaverage intellectual functioning" indicates an intelligence quotient (IQ) below 68–70. "Adaptive skill areas" include the skills needed for personal independence and social responsibility (for example, dressing, using the toilet, eating, controlling behavior, having independence in the community, and interacting with peers).

The *DSM-IV* recognizes the following four levels of mental retardation (see Table 1):

- mild mental retardation: IQ level from 50–55 to approximately 70
- moderate mental retardation: IQ level from 35–40 to 50–55
- severe mental retardation: IQ level from 20–25 to 25–40
- profound mental retardation: IQ below 20–25

Table 1
Levels of Intelligence (Normal and Below)

Level of Intelligence	Intelligence Test Score	% of Population
Normal	85–115	68
Borderline	70–84	14
Mild mental retardation	50–69	2
Moderate mental retardation	35–54	<0.5
Severe mental retardation	20–39	<0.25
Profound mental retardation	<20–25	<0.25

Note: Scores overlap between the levels, and the diagnosis of a particular level of retardation will be determined in part by the individual's actual level of functioning in society.

MILD MENTAL RETARDATION

Although children who have mild mental retardation typically learn more slowly in school than do children with normal IQs, their condition may not be noticeable in nonacademic settings. As they grow older, they are capable of taking responsibility for their basic, day-to-day needs and usually develop adequate social and communication skills. By their late teens, these children generally reach about a sixth-grade level of academic achievement. Although their choice of careers is somewhat limited, with adequate supervision and support from family and community, they are capable of earning a living successfully. According to the *DSM-IV*, about 85 percent of all mentally retarded people have mild mental retardation.

MODERATE MENTAL RETARDATION

Children with moderate mental retardation can usually be expected to learn the communication skills they need to interact with others. At the elementary school level, their curriculum generally concentrates on the basic academic skills necessary for daily life, such as reading, adding and subtracting, telling time, and handling money. Their academic skills are not likely to go much beyond the second-grade level. As they grow older, their school programs typically focus on basic self-help skills. As adults, they can often find successful vocations in sheltered workshops or supervised work settings. In their home lives, they generally need supervision in either a family or group home setting. The *DSM-IV* estimates that about 9 to 11 percent of all mentally retarded people have moderate mental retardation.

SEVERE MENTAL RETARDATION

According to H. W. Moser, C. T. Ramey, and C. O. Leonard in their essay "Mental Retardation," 35 to 60 percent of the instances of severe mental retardation are caused by genetic abnormalities. Children with severe mental retardation are often found to have other disabilities as well (for example, speech and language problems). Their school programs typically concentrate on basic self-care skills, communication, and social interaction. The curriculum may also include familiarity with the alphabet, simple counting, and some sight reading of important words, such as "entrance," "exit," "men," "women," "walk," and "don't walk." As adults, people with severe mental retardation usually do well in supervised settings, either with their families or in group homes. In some cases, however, an associated medical problem may make it necessary for them to live in a nursing facility. According to the *DSM-IV*, about 3 or 4 percent of all mentally retarded people have severe mental retardation.

INTELLIGENCE QUOTIENT (IQ)

A person's intelligence quotient, or IQ, is assessed by a standardized, individually administered test. The Wechsler Intelligence Scales for Children, Third Edition (WISC-III), the Stanford-Binet test, and the Kaufman Assessment Battery for Children are examples of intelligence tests that may be used to evaluate children. The results allow the test administrator to assign a score that estimates intelligence. It's important to keep in mind, however, that IQ tests measure mainly the ability to perform in school, rather than the ability to perform life functions. Social and cultural background and native language can influence IQ scores, as can sensory, physical movement, and communication disabilities.

PROFOUND MENTAL RETARDATION

Profound mental retardation is rare, according to Moser, Ramey, and Leonard in "Mental Retardation." Only about 1 in every 2,000 children is profoundly retarded. According to the *DSM-IV*, for most children who are diagnosed with this level of mental retardation, a neurological condition accounts for the disorder. As young children, individuals with profound retardation typically have problems sensing the world around them, and they have difficulty moving around. As they grow older, they generally learn best in a very structured environment with constant help and supervision from a caregiver. This sort of training can help them improve their motor development, their ability to care for themselves, and their speech. As adults, they may be able to perform simple tasks in well-supervised work settings. According to *DSM-IV* statistics, about 1 to 2 percent of all mentally retarded people have profound mental retardation.

CAUSES

When parents have a mentally retarded child, one of the questions they usually ask is, "Why is this child the way he or she is?" Unfortunately, there are often no clear answers. According to Maxmen and Ward's *Essential Psychopathology and Its Treatment*, the specific cause of mental retardation in children can be identified in only 25 to 50 percent of all cases. When the causes can be determined, they are usually found before, during, or shortly after birth.

Possible causes of mental retardation include the following:

- accidents that cause brain damage
- birth injury or lack of oxygen during delivery
- certain infections during pregnancy
- complications of premature birth
- glandular problems (for example, hypothyroidism)
- inherited (genetic) disorders or *chromosome* defects (a chromosome is a strand of matter in the nucleus of a cell that contains the individual's genetic information)
- malnutrition before and after birth during essential periods of the baby's brain development
- severe bleeding at birth

- toxins that affect the brain (for example, lead poisoning)
- use of certain drugs or alcohol during pregnancy

Because so many of these causes have their roots in pregnancy and delivery, adequate medical care and nutrition throughout pregnancy are essential.

CHROMOSOME PROBLEMS

All human cells except sperm and egg cells normally contain 46 chromosomes (sperm and egg cells contain 23 chromosomes each). The chromosomes are arranged in pairs, with the 23rd pair containing the sex chromosomes: X (female) and Y (male). When a baby is conceived, genetic mistakes can sometimes result in the inclusion of too much or too little chromosome material. In these cases, the outcome for the child will depend on which chromosome is affected.

Scientists do not yet understand completely why these chromosomal irregularities occur. They do know, however, that the defects can be inherited. There are also indications that they may occur more frequently in children born of older parents.

Down Syndrome

A Down syndrome child, like Matthew Smith, has an extra chromosome (called a trisomy) on the 21st pair. In other words, he has 47 chromosomes instead of 46. This is the most common cause of mental retardation—Moser, Ramey, and Leonard's article "Mental Retardation" estimates that it accounts for about 30 percent of all cases. According to these researchers, approximately 1 out of every 800 to 1,000 live births will be a Down syndrome child.

Down syndrome children have a distinctive appearance. The backs of their heads are flat, and they have slanted eyes with skin folds at the inner corners. (For this reason, they were once referred to as Mongoloids.) These children have small noses and ears and unusually tiny hands and feet. Their muscle strength is generally less than that of the average child in the same age group.

About one-third of children who have Down syndrome also suffer from congenital heart disease. They are sometimes born with other physical defects, such as bowel blockage. In the past, many Down syndrome children died from these medical complications. Today, however, the life expectancy of a child with this condition is usually from 50 to 60 years.

Slanted eyes, small ears, and a small nose are telltale signs of Down syndrome. People with this disorder also suffer from mild to severe mental retardation and may experience other physical complications as well.

The level of intelligence of children with Down syndrome varies from person to person. An individual with Down syndrome can range in functioning from severe mental retardation to low-average intelligence. Although every individual is unique, most children with Down syndrome are sociable and affectionate youngsters.

Fragile-X Syndrome

Fragile-X syndrome is the second most common genetic cause of mental retardation. According to the *American Psychiatric Press Textbook of Psychiatry*, this condition occurs in 1 out of every 1,000 males.

In individuals with this syndrome, one of the X chromosomes will appear to be weak or fragile. Because girls have two X chromosomes and boys have an X and a Y, girls seem to be protected from this syndrome—if one X chromosome is weak, the other is usually healthy enough to compensate. Fragile-X syndrome is therefore generally seen only in males. Children with this condition are mildly to severely mentally retarded. They typically have abnormal facial features, including large jaws, foreheads, and ears. They are often hyperactive and resist changes in their environment. They may have attention deficits (see chapter 5) and difficulty articulating words. According to Moser, Ramey, and Leonard's "Mental Retardation," about 20 to 40 percent of children with fragile-X syndrome show symptoms of autism (see chapter 4). Girls who carry this chromosome may have *learning disorders* (see chapter 3) or mild mental retardation.

Cri du Chat Syndrome

Cri du chat syndrome is a rare genetic cause of mental retardation. According to Moser, Ramey, and Leonard's "Mental Retardation," it occurs in only 1 out of every 20,000 live births. Children with this syndrome make a distinctive noise similar to a cat's cry, and they are usually severely retarded. These youngsters are typically small and grow slowly. Their heads are generally little and round, and their faces lack symmetry. Their eyes are typically wide set, with skin folds on the inner lids. Children with cri du chat syndrome usually learn to walk, but their language development is generally poor.

Trisomy 13 and Trisomy 18

Children with trisomy 13 and trisomy 18 have extra genetic material in their 13th or 18th chromosomes. Individuals who are born with either of these rare disorders are typically profoundly retarded, and most do not live past their first year. They are generally small and weak, and most have additional medical problems. For example, they sometimes suffer from congenital heart disease, *apnea* (a pause in normal breathing), or seizures.

INTRAUTERINE CAUSES

Intrauterine causes of mental retardation occur during pregnancy, when the child is still in the mother's uterus. The three most common intrauterine causes are asphyxia, fetal alcohol syndrome, and infections.

Asphyxia occurs when the baby doesn't get enough oxygen. Causes

THE HISTORY OF
MENTAL RETARDATION

In the 14th and 15th centuries in Europe, people who were mentally retarded were sometimes looked upon as "holy infants" blessed by God. During the Reformation, however, Martin Luther referred to mentally retarded people as "feebleminded" and "Godless." He wrote that society should rid itself of the burden of these individuals.

In the early 20th century in France, Alfred Binet developed the first psychometric tests (*psychometric* refers to the psychological technique of mental measurement) to measure human intellectual capacity. Unfortunately, these tests were often used to identify "imbeciles" and exclude these children from school.

Then in 1934, Norwegian researcher Asbjørn Følling discovered *phenylketonuria* (an inherited metabolic disease that prevents the metabolization of the amino acid phenylalanine), an illness that can cause mental retardation. Because phenylketonuria is treatable, the scientific study of mental retardation finally became accepted.

The French scientist Alfred Binet (1857–1911) devised the first test to measure the relative intellectual capacity of children—what became known in America as the IQ test. Binet's ideas were later misused to justify discrimination against people on the basis of intelligence.

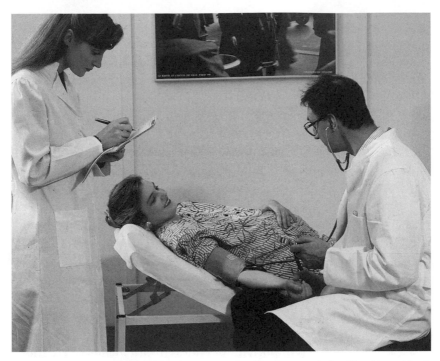

A pregnant woman with high blood pressure or toxic substances in her blood is at risk of giving birth to a mentally retarded child. This woman is reducing that risk by receiving regular prenatal checkups.

include *hypertension* (high blood pressure) or *toxemia* in the mother (toxemia is an abnormal condition during pregnancy in which the kidneys fail to work efficiently and toxic substances accumulate in the blood) or *placenta previa* (when the baby's placenta becomes detached from the uterine wall).

Fetal alcohol syndrome occurs when the mother exposes her unborn child to high levels of alcohol. This can result in mild mental retardation and often includes symptoms of *attention-deficit/hyperactivity disorder* (ADHD) as well (see chapter 5). Children with this syndrome tend to be small, with narrow eyes, flat cheeks, short noses, and thin upper lips. According to Maxmen and Ward's *Essential Psychopathology and Its Treatment*, this condition occurs in as many as 1 out of every 600 live births.

Two fairly common infections that can cause mental retardation are rubella (or measles) and toxoplasmosis, a disease often acquired from cats.

TREATMENT

In most cases, children do not outgrow mental retardation. In their essay "Autism and Mental Retardation," Wendy Stone, William E. MacLean Jr., and Kerry L. Hogan state that "mental retardation is an enduring disability, one that for most persons is lifelong." As progress is made in treatment and therapy, however, the outlook for many individuals has become brighter. According to the *American Psychiatric Press Textbook of Psychiatry*, "about two-thirds of mentally retarded individuals shed their diagnosis in adulthood as adaptive skills increase. . . . Generally, adaptive behavior increases over the course of a lifetime."

Perhaps the most important factor for effective treatment is a set of realistic expectations for the mentally retarded child. When expectations—on the part of the parents, the child, or teachers—are set too high, the child can become frustrated and discouraged. Conversely, expectations that are set too low can damage the child's self-esteem and sense of hope and can become a self-fulfilling prophecy. That is, the child who is told that he or she will never amount to much of anything probably won't.

Early intervention is important for children with mental retardation, and in most cases the most significant treatment—teaching the children life skills—is provided by the public school system. Thanks to recent legislation (see chapter 1), all children are guaranteed a free and appropriate education. In a school setting, most mentally retarded children can learn the academic, social, and self-help skills that they will need in order to function successfully in life.

Children who are severely or profoundly retarded sometimes require drug therapy in addition to skill training. Medication can help the individuals better manage their behavior and their emotions.

In the past, society tended to focus on the lower academic abilities of people with mental retardation. Today, however, social and interpersonal skills are being given greater importance. Professionals are working more to help mentally retarded individuals develop the talents they do have, rather than concentrating on their deficiencies. As a result, mental health workers are relying less on intelligence tests as an assessment tool. In education, greater emphasis is also being placed on vocational training, and more and more schools are connecting with businesses and industries in an attempt to help children with mental retardation work toward becoming self-supporting.

In the past, society may have looked upon treatment for mentally retarded individuals as charity. Today we consider such treatment to be their right. In 1971, the United Nations Declaration on the Rights of Mentally Retarded Individuals stated that people with mental retardation have the right to "medical care, physical therapy, and the education, training, rehabilitation, and guidance needed to develop the individual's potential." U.S. courts now look to the U.N. declaration as they include individuals with mental retardation under the Constitution's protection of individual rights. Once Down syndrome children such as Matthew Smith were denied lifesaving medical treatment, and neglect and abuse were tolerated. Today mentally retarded individuals are represented by their own self-advocacy group.

In the article "Aging Parents with Mentally Retarded Children," by M. M. Seltzer and M. W. Krauss, one mother had this to say about her mentally retarded youngster, "This child has taught me an appreciation for the little things in life we take for granted. My other children learned about love and caring from [my child with mental retardation]. I don't ask, 'Why me?' I ask, 'Why not me?'" The following words of wisdom for parents of mentally retarded children came from another parent: "My advice is to value who he is, not who he isn't."

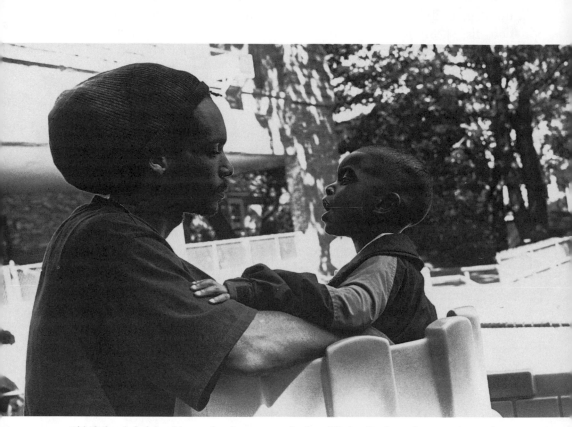

This father is helping his son develop communication skills by simply paying attention and responding to him. Parents are usually the first to discover if their children are having problems learning. Whether a problem constitutes a genuine disorder, however, is a matter best decided by health specialists.

3

LEARNING, MOTOR SKILLS, AND COMMUNICATION DISORDERS

Albert had a hard time in school. In fact, he couldn't even speak correctly until he was nine years old. His teachers assumed he was a "slow learner." He found math difficult, and labored over the solution to any problem. When Albert's father asked the headmaster of his school what might be a good future career for his son, the headmaster replied, "Albert will never make a success of anything."

Like Albert, Thomas also had difficulty in school. He was too impulsive, and his impulses often got him into trouble. Thomas's teacher referred to him as "addled." Even Thomas's father agreed with that description. Thomas became so discouraged that he was convinced he must be a dunce.

As it turned out, Albert and Thomas both had learning disorders. Although not every child with a learning disorder grows up to be a brilliant mathematician like Albert Einstein or an ingenious inventor like Thomas Edison, having a learning disorder is not a negative reflection of a child's intelligence. It means only that the child may face challenges in the average school setting.

WHAT ARE LEARNING DISORDERS?

According to the *DSM-IV*, a learning disorder should be diagnosed whenever an individual's achievement on individually administered, standardized tests in reading, mathematics, or written expression is substantially below that expected for age, schooling, and level of intelligence. In these cases, learning problems get in the way of achievements that require reading, mathematics, or writing skills.

Children diagnosed with these disorders often have communication or motor skills disorders as well. They may also suffer from attention-deficit/hyperactivity disorder, conduct disorder, or oppositional defiant disorder. According to the *American Psychiatric Press Textbook of Psychiatry*, approximately 5 percent of all school-aged children in the United States have been identified as having a learning disorder.

The *DSM-IV* lists the following four types of learning disorders: reading disorder, mathematics disorder, disorder of written expression, and learning disorder not otherwise specified.

READING DISORDER

Children with reading disorder, which is also called *dyslexia*, are slow to learn to read. Compared to other children their age, they have difficulty understanding the meaning of the words that they do read, they miss many words altogether, and they are apt to reverse the letters of a word. (For instance, they may read "dog" instead of "god" or "was" instead of "saw," or they may reverse the letters themselves and read "bab" instead of "dad.") Most children with reading disorder also have disorder of written expression. According to the *DSM-IV*, 4 percent of school-age children have dyslexia, and from 60 to 80 percent of all children diagnosed with this disorder are boys.

MATHEMATICS DISORDER

Most children who have mathematics disorder also have reading disorder. Children with mathematics disorder have a hard time learning to count. They find simple addition and subtraction calculations difficult, and they are often unable to create a mental image of sets of objects. Frequently, they have problems thinking in terms of right and left, up and down, or east and west. They may have trouble sequencing items in a specific order. According to the *DSM-IV*, about 6 percent of the population has mathematics disorder.

DISORDER OF WRITTEN EXPRESSION

Most children with disorder of written expression also have reading disorder. They have trouble with spelling, grammar, and punctuation. They find it difficult to form sentences and paragraphs, and they tend to write slowly and illegibly. These children may also have a motor disability that causes problems with *fine motor coordination* (control of the small muscles in the hands), making it even more difficult for them to write neatly. Their school papers are typically full of erased and crossed-out words. Children with this disorder sometimes write their letters backwards—they may even write entire words or sentences in reverse order. All children experience these problems to some degree as they learn to write. But the child with a disorder of written expression continues to struggle after other children in the same age group have successfully mastered these writing skills.

Most children with learning disorders are smart enough to handle the strategies needed to cope with them. The earlier the problem is detected, the more opportunity the child has to practice these strategies, and the more successful therapy will be. Here a tutor helps a young boy with his reading.

LEARNING DISORDERS NOT OTHERWISE SPECIFIED

Children with learning disorders not otherwise specified are those who do not have a significant problem in any one area of learning but have some difficulties in the areas of reading, math, and writing that, when taken together, interfere with their academic achievement.

CAUSES OF LEARNING DISORDERS

A learning disorder can occur when a small area of the brain functions abnormally. Whether a problem is considered a learning disorder or not is a question of degree. Each individual's brain works differently from everyone else's. However, when a neurological abnormality interferes with a person's ability to achieve, particularly in a school setting, a learning disorder is diagnosed. Learning disorders can be caused by birth trauma, by genetics, or by minimal brain damage that results from accidents or drugs either before or after birth. Children with these disorders cover the same range of intelligence as the rest of the population. However, they lack the ability to perform specific skills as expected according to their level of intelligence.

Successful learning requires that we first be able to input information. Then we must integrate or understand the data. Next we have to store the information in our memories. And last, we must be able to output the data, expressing what we have learned. Children with a learning disorder have difficulty with one or more of these steps.

If a child cannot correctly perceive written shapes, for example, then he or she will not be able to input the information contained in the writing. Reading requires that our eyes focus on specific letters or groups of letters and then track from left to right, line after line. Children with a reading disorder may skip over words, read the same line twice, or skip lines. They may be unable to distinguish the shapes of letters, or they may be unable to focus on the letters rather than on the white spaces around them. This does not mean that there is something wrong with their eyes. Rather, it means that their brains have difficulty inputting written data.

If a child has trouble with the integration step of the learning process, then he or she may be unable to sequence, abstract, or organize. These skills are necessary components of mathematic operations. They also play an important part in making sense out of a story or writing a paragraph. Children who cannot sequence easily may have trouble learning to count or saying the alphabet. They may have a hard time learning the days of the week or the months of the year.

Similarly, a child who has difficulty making abstractions may approach everything from a completely literal point of view. The youngster may be unable to apply to a new situation what he or she has learned. The child may view facts only in the precise situation in which they were first presented and may be completely unable to make generalizations. A child who cannot organize information may be unable to put together into a single picture what he or she has learned.

Children who have trouble with the memory step of learning frequently perform poorly on tests. If their short-term memory is such

FAMOUS PEOPLE WITH LEARNING DISORDERS

The following list includes a few of the many people with learning disorders who have achieved great success:

Hans Christian Andersen, *writer*
Harry Belafonte, *singer and actor*
Alexander Graham Bell, *inventor*
George Burns, *comedian*
Cher, *singer and actor*
Winston Churchill, *statesman*
Leonardo da Vinci, *painter*
Walt Disney, *film producer*
Thomas Edison, *inventor*
Albert Einstein, *physicist*

Henry Ford, *industrialist*
Danny Glover, *actor*
Whoopi Goldberg, *comedian and actor*
Jay Leno, *comedian*
George Patton, *U.S. Army general*
Nelson Rockefeller, *U.S. vice president*
Woodrow Wilson, *U.S. president*
William Butler Yeats, *poet*

Thomas Edison became one of the greatest inventors of all time, but as a child he had so much trouble concentrating that his teachers called him "addled" and he had to leave school. Some experts believe that if Edison were growing up today, he would be diagnosed with attention-deficit disorder.

that they can't remember what they have read from one paragraph to the next, or what the teacher said five minutes before, then their learning will be even more impaired.

A child who has difficulty with the output level of learning may have disorder of written expression. The youngster may show signs of motor skills disorder or communication disorder as well.

MOTOR SKILLS DISORDER

Motor skills disorder seldom occurs alone. It almost always accompanies one of the *DSM-IV* categories of learning disorders or another psychological condition. Children with motor skills disorder move clumsily because they have trouble coordinating their muscle movements. According to the *American Psychiatric Press Textbook of Psychiatry*, about 5 percent of all children have significant problems with *gross motor skills* (coordination of the large muscles in the arms, legs, and body) or with fine motor coordination. Because athletic ability is valued highly in our culture, children with this disorder may suffer from poor self-esteem. They may dread going to physical education class, and they may try to avoid any activity that would highlight their problem.

COMMUNICATION DISORDERS

According to the *American Psychiatric Press Textbook of Psychiatry*, about 15 percent of all school-aged children have a speech problem— that is, difficulty producing the actual sounds of the language. Another 6 percent struggle with language (communicating meaning). About 50 percent of these children have some additional psychological disorder, and 20 percent have a learning disorder. The *DSM-IV* lists the following categories of communication disorders: expressive language disorder, mixed receptive-expressive language disorder, phonological disorder, and stuttering.

Children with expressive language disorder may have a limited vocabulary and speak in short sentences. They are likely to find it difficult to learn new words and use words correctly. They may order their words in an odd manner or leave out elements of sentences, such as the noun or the verb.

Mixed receptive-expressive language disorder involves the same symptoms as expressive language disorder. In addition, however, these children have problems understanding language that is spoken to them.

Language disorders can interfere greatly with achievement at school. When called upon to address their classmates, as this girl is doing, students with such disorders may stutter, repeat the same words over and over, or have trouble forming complete sentences.

Children with phonological disorder fail to articulate certain speech sounds. They may lisp or mispronounce other letter sounds at an age when other children have mastered these skills.

Children who stutter repeat sounds or entire words. Vocalization may fill these youngsters with tension and anxiety. Blinking, jerking, or fist clenching often accompany the stuttering.

With each of the communication disorders, the child's trouble communicating information to others makes academic achievement difficult.

TREATMENT OF LEARNING DISORDERS

Parents who suspect that their child has a learning disorder should seek professional diagnosis as the first step toward treatment. Because these disorders are most obvious in school settings, low achievement in a particular subject is usually the first indication of a problem. An otherwise bright child may become more and more frustrated in math class. Or a youngster may do well when tested on material that he or she has been taught orally yet fall behind whenever he or she is required to read a lesson.

Although federal laws (see chapter 1) guarantee each child a free and "appropriate" education, each state and school system has its own procedure for carrying out this legislation. Basically, however, Public Law 94-142 guarantees that the following steps will be implemented:

1. *Search:* Each school system will have a procedure for identifying students who may have a disability. This means that, when parents and teachers suspect that a child has a learning disorder, they can refer the youngster to the school psychologist for diagnostic testing.

2. *Find:* A system is in place for collecting information and designing an evaluation once a student with a potential problem has been identified.

3. *Evaluation:* A comprehensive and multidisciplinary evaluation takes place. This involves the school psychologist as well as teachers and other school personnel.

4. *Conference:* Parents or guardians meet with school personnel to review the conclusions of the evaluation, any diagnoses established, any proposed placement, and the individualized education plan (IEP). All this is recorded in writing.

5. *Parents' decision process:* Parents or guardians decide to accept, request explanations for or changes to, or reject the proposed placement and IEP.

6. *Appeals process:* If parents reject the diagnosis, placement recommendation, or IEP, an appeals process begins with the local school and can go from there to the county or state level.

7. *Follow-up:* Progress reports are provided to the family, and a formal reevaluation is made every three years (sooner if requested by parents or teachers). Steps 5 and 6 are then repeated before implementing the next year's plan.

Perhaps not all children with learning disorders will grow up to be famous thinkers like Einstein and Edison, but there is no reason why they can't become happy, productive, successful adults. If their problems are not addressed, however, they can suffer from poor self-esteem or become discouraged and frustrated in the school setting. Their frustration can then lead to other problems. Because these children find it difficult to succeed at the skills that they have been told are so important for achievement, they sometimes give up. Some may even turn to delinquency or violence to vent their frustration.

For this reason, early diagnosis is essential to the effective treatment of learning disorders. The more opportunities a child is given to practice successful strategies for coping with learning disorders, the more the child will become accustomed to performing these strategies automatically. In *The Practice of Child Therapy*, authors Richard J. Morris and Thomas R. Kratochwill compare learning to any other skill: "Basketball players practice jump shots over and over again; musicians practice short musical selections repeatedly. Their goal is to develop skills to a level of fluid accuracy. With enough practice, they do not have to devote much attention to the mechanics of their skills."

In most cases, children with learning disorders have more than adequate intelligence to learn these coping strategies. Their own unique and creative slant on life may even come to enrich their learning.

In the movie Rain Man, *Dustin Hoffman plays an autistic adult with a phenomenal memory that allows him to recall the contents of entire phone books. When his brother, played by Tom Cruise, asks him to board an airplane, he flies into a panic because he can remember every airline disaster in history.*

4
PERVASIVE DEVELOPMENTAL DISORDERS

The hero of The Who's rock opera *Tommy* is a strange boy who "doesn't know what day it is. . . . Surrounded by his friends, he sits so silently, and unaware of everything." Tommy seems unable to see and feel the world around him. His father wonders, "Has he ever heard a word I said?" And yet strangely, Tommy is a "pinball wizard." Even though he acts as though he is deaf, mute, and blind, he "sure plays a mean pinball."

Pete Townshend, the composer of *Tommy*, has indicated that the hero of his rock opera is autistic. In the language of the *DSM-IV*, Tommy has a *pervasive developmental disorder*.

WHAT IS A PERVASIVE DEVELOPMENTAL DISORDER?

The *DSM-IV* defines *pervasive developmental disorder* as a "severe and pervasive impairment in several areas of development," including social interaction and communication skills. In addition, a child with this condition may engage in rigid and repetitive behaviors and interests. The *DSM-IV* lists four types of pervasive developmental disorders: autistic disorder, Asperger's disorder, childhood disintegrative disorder, and Rett's disorder.

Children with pervasive developmental disorders sometimes have multiple disabilities. Many of them are mentally retarded. However, unlike simple mental retardation, pervasive developmental disorders are not characterized simply by slow or limited development but by development that is "deviant" or "abnormal." Children with these disorders function very differently from other individuals. Like Tommy, they seem to be in their own world, unable to communicate with the world around them.

AUTISTIC DISORDER

Leo Kanner, an American psychologist working in Baltimore, first described autism in 1943. In his practice, he noticed several children who seemed unable to experience normal emotional ties to other people. Kanner noticed the following characteristics of these children:

- "The outstanding . . . disorder is the children's inability to relate themselves in the ordinary way to people and situations. . . . Profound aloneness dominates all behavior."

- "He has good relation to objects; he is interested in them, can play with them happily for hours. . . . The child's relation to people is altogether different."

- "The child's noises and motions and all his performances are as monotonously repetitious as are his verbal utterances. . . . The child's behavior is governed by an anxiously obsessive desire for the maintenance of sameness."

- "The astounding vocabulary of the speaking children, the excellent memory for events of several years before, the phenomenal rote memory for poems and names, and the precise recollection of complex patterns and sequences bespeak good intelligence."

When researchers first studied autism, many believed that the disorder was the result of a "cold" mother. Current findings have dispelled that notion. Uta Frith, author of *Autism*, among other books on the subject, observes, "Autistic children are not made autistic by parents who did not love them enough. Autism is a rare and tragic event that can hit anyone, any family, without warning. Its biological origin is likely to be well before birth." According to the *DSM-IV*, 2 to 5 out of every 10,000 children are autistic.

In *Autism*, Frith tells the story of an autistic boy named Peter, a much-loved child from a normal, healthy family. In the first year of Peter's life, he did not seem any different from any other baby. His mother noted that he seemed to cry and laugh for much the same reasons that his older sister had at the same age.

When Peter became a toddler, however, his parents began to worry about him. Unlike his sister, who had started to talk at a year, Peter said no words at all until he was much older. Even worse, he didn't seem to understand anything that was said to him. He didn't even look up when his name was called, and he showed no interest in listening to people speak. He never stretched out his arms to be picked up, and he seemed

Autistic children have difficulty interacting with people, but many show enormous empathy for animals. In addition, the warmth, soft texture, and gentle noises of a cat or other small animal can have a calming effect on an autistic child.

perfectly happy to sit all by himself examining the tiny details of his building blocks.

At first, Peter's family assumed that he was simply a very independent and self-sufficient child whose talking was somewhat delayed. Eventually his grandmother suggested that his hearing be tested.

Autistic children often exhibit an astonishing capacity to master puzzles, chess, and other games, though they may have problems performing much simpler tasks. Here a young girl quickly assembles a jigsaw puzzle.

Perhaps deafness would explain why Peter seemed to inhabit his own small world.

Soon, however, Peter began to respond to sounds, even though he didn't respond to voices. He was terrified by the noise of the vacuum cleaner, and he would rush to the window whenever he heard a bus go by. Clearly, he was not deaf.

By Peter's third year, though, his parents knew that something else was seriously wrong. He showed no interest in other children his age, and he still did not talk. Instead of playing with his little toy cars, he would put them in long straight lines. The spinning wheels of the cars also fascinated him. He loved music and would listen to Antonio Vivaldi's "Four Seasons" endlessly. Sometimes he would burst into laughter, and other times he would have a violent tantrum, but his family could never understand the reason behind his emotions. He was an expert at jigsaw puzzles—to his family's amazement, he could even do them picture-side down.

Peter's mother had heard of autism, but his family dismissed the possibility of this diagnosis for Peter. They had heard that autistic people were often retarded and that they were incapable of showing any attachment to others. In many ways, Peter seemed very bright. He also preferred to be near to his family and enjoyed playing rough-and-tumble games with his father. To Peter's parents' dismay, however, when he was three years old, he was diagnosed as autistic.

The next few years were difficult for Peter's family. Since he had no language skills, they couldn't explain anything to him and he was very difficult to manage. He hated any changes in his routine, and he didn't like to leave the house. On the street or in a store, he would often make a high-pitched noise and jump up and down.

When Peter was five years old, however, he started to become easier to handle. He developed some language skills, although he often echoed the phrases of others and spoke in a strange sing-song voice. His vocabulary was also odd. For instance, he knew the meaning of the word *dodecahedron* but seemed unable to understand the word *think*.

Peter did well at a special school for autistic children. He learned to read, write, and perform mathematical operations. He loved to draw and showed some artistic talent. He also memorized all the London bus routes by number and destination, and he began collecting anything that had to do with buses. He talked a lot now, but he tended to make such statements as "Today is Monday, yesterday was Sunday, and tomorrow is Tuesday." And when he was badly injured after a fall, he didn't mention it to anyone. His mother was horrified to discover blood on his clothes when she did the laundry.

As a teenager, Peter began to ask repeatedly, "Am I right? Am I a good boy?" This was an indication that he cared what others thought of him. But the annoying frequency of the questions showed that he was unable to read people's reactions to his behavior. He was tall and good-looking now, but his movements were awkward, and his voice was loud and squeaky. He often grimaced and twisted his hands, and he didn't adjust his behavior according to different situations. For example, he was apt to pick his nose thoroughly in the midst of a conversation with someone.

At this point in his life, Peter understood that he was different, but he couldn't understand how and why. He sometimes experienced periods of frustration and unhappiness. His understanding was extremely literal, and he couldn't comprehend explanations of emotional states. When his mother once remarked that his sister was crying her eyes out, Peter looked for the eyes on the floor.

Peter is now in his thirties and still lives at home. He is often restless and pesters others with his endless repetitive talk. But he enjoys watching television, he helps his mother with gardening and household chores, and every day he paces the lawn on exactly the same track. His parents appreciate that he has come a long way from the days when he seemed totally unaware of others, but they worry about what will happen to him when they are no longer around to look after him.

Peter's story, as Frith points out, shows that autism looks different at different ages. Children with autism make progress. They learn and adapt. However, according to Frith, "Mental development is not only distorted and delayed but, if its aim is maturity, then this aim is never reached. . . . Autism, like mental retardation, does not go away, despite changes in behavior."

ASPERGER'S DISORDER

Asperger's disorder is considered a subcategory of autism, a somewhat milder form of a more severe disorder. Asperger's disorder is far more common than autism, however. According to Tony Attwood, author of *Asperger's Syndrome*, the condition is now being diagnosed in children who, in the past, would never have been considered autistic.

Attwood lists the following social impairments as typical of a child with Asperger's disorder: an inability and a lack of desire to interact with peers, an absence of appreciation of social cues, and socially and emotionally inappropriate behaviors. He also lists the following nonverbal behaviors as common in children with this condition: the limited use of gestures; clumsy body language; the limited or inappropriate use of facial expressions; and a peculiar, stiff gaze.

Although children with Asperger's disorder typically have great difficulty functioning socially, they possess many intellectual abilities. Their long-term memory banks are often enormous. They can, for instance, remember the smallest details about their fields of interest. They tend to have one-track minds, and their thinking is often rigid and inflexible. But according to the article "Autism with Hyperlexia," by E. Tirosh and J. Canby, many children with Asperger's disorder have incredible vocabularies. Even so, however, they may have difficulty understanding what a story means. Children with this condition tend to do very well in

The Dutch painter Vincent van Gogh (1853–1890) displayed many of the traits now associated with Asperger's disorder: socially inappropriate behavior, extreme eccentricity, and a brilliantly vivid imagination.

elementary school but not as well in secondary school, when comprehension, problem solving, and teamwork often become important for academic achievement.

Children with Asperger's disorder generally have vivid imaginations. However, whereas other youngsters might act out the roles of favorite fairy tale or television show characters, these children often pretend to be objects rather than people or animals. According to Attwood in *Asperger's Syndrome*, "One boy spent many minutes rocking from side to side. When asked what he was doing, he replied, 'I'm car wiper blades'—his current special interest. One boy pretended to be a teapot, while a girl spent several weeks pretending to be a blocked toilet!"

Because school curricula tend to depend on verbal thinking whereas individuals with Asperger's disorder tend to excel in visual thinking, children with this condition may be at a particular disadvantage in the school environment. They are, however, inclined to do well at games such as chess and in the fields of art and science.

Attwood has this to say about people with Asperger's disorder: "Digby Tantam [clinical professor of psychotherapy at the University of Sheffield in England] has used the term 'lifelong eccentricity' to describe the long-term outcome of individuals with Asperger's Syndrome. The term 'eccentricity' is not used in a derogatory sense. In this author's opinion, they are a bright thread in the rich tapestry of life. Our civilization would be extremely dull and sterile if we did not have and treasure people with Asperger's Syndrome."

CHILDHOOD DISINTEGRATIVE DISORDER

The *DSM-IV* defines childhood disintegrative disorder as "a marked regression in multiple areas of functioning following a period of at least 2 years of normal development." Somewhere between ages 2 and 10, children with this disorder begin to lose the skills they have learned in at least two of the following areas:

- bowel or bladder control
- expressive or receptive language
- motor skills
- play
- social skills

After the onset of this disorder, children show many of the same symptoms as autism. However, unlike autism, childhood disintegrative disorder is usually accompanied by severe mental retardation.

RETT'S DISORDER

Like youngsters with childhood disintegrative disorder, children with Rett's disorder begin life with a period of normal functioning. Between the ages of 5 and 30 months, however, these children lose any skills they have acquired and all interest in interacting with those around them. Their physical growth begins to slow, and their intellectual and social functioning deteriorates. Until the age of three or four, these children may appear to be autistic or to have childhood disintegrative disorder. At this point, however, increasingly severe neurological symptoms appear. Their muscles become weak and spastic, and they are often eventually confined to wheelchairs.

According to the *DSM-IV*, this is a rare disorder that has been reported only in girls. The *American Psychiatric Press Textbook of Psychiatry* indicates that the condition occurs in 5 to 15 out of every 100,000 girls. Children with this disorder all engage in a strange movement that looks as though they are continually washing their hands.

CAUSES OF PERVASIVE DEVELOPMENTAL DISORDERS

Scientists are still unclear about the specific causes of pervasive developmental disorders. According to Maxmen and Ward's *Essential Psychopathology and Its Treatment*, research indicates that there is some genetic basis for autism. As much as 10 percent of autistic conditions may be caused by the mother's development of the rubella infection during pregnancy. Specific medical problems, such as lack of oxygen during birth, neurological infections, encephalitis, and untreated phenylketonuria can cause these disorders as well. At birth, children with these conditions also have more complications and congenital malformations.

In an article in the *American Journal of Psychiatry*, researchers H. J. Garber and and E. R. Ritvo report that brain scans of adults with these disorders indicate that brain structure is normal. However, in *Essential Psychopathology and Its Treatment* Maxmen and Ward report abnormalities in the chemicals that carry messages from neuron to neuron within the brain. In their essay "Autism and Mental Retardation," moreover, Stone, MacLean, and Hogan conclude that these disorders are caused by abnormalities in the central nervous system.

TREATMENT OF PERVASIVE DEVELOPMENTAL DISORDERS

Treatment of pervasive developmental disorders depends on the severity of the particular individual's condition as well as on whether the condition is accompanied by mental retardation or another disorder. For all types of developmental disorders, however, a carefully structured program is essential.

In *The Treatment of Psychiatric Disorders*, Reid and Balis indicate that

Therapy for autistic children includes lessons in play and social interaction. Therapists may also use touch, as shown here, to break through the profound feelings of isolation autistic children experience.

the most effective treatment programs for these disorders involve *behavior modification* (a technique that uses reinforcement to encourage desirable behaviors and discourage undesirable behaviors). These programs are most effective when they include both the child's school and home environments. Early intervention is an important factor in effective treatment. That is, the younger the child when he or she begins treatment, the better chance the youngster has for a successful long-term outcome. Reid and Balis also report that music therapy has been shown to encourage social communication and improved attention and that drug therapy has proved to have little effect on these disorders.

Although pervasive developmental disorders are lifelong conditions, Frith has this to say in her book *Autism*:

> Autistic people can, and often do, compensate for their handicap to a remarkable degree. They may be guided to a niche in society where their assets are put to good use. They may remain at home as helpful companions to aging parents who understand them. There are less favorable outcomes. However, one must remember that to predict the future of an individual autistic child is just as uncertain as it is in the case of a normal child.

Dr. Michael D. Powers concludes his book *Children with Autism* with this advice to parents of children with this disorder: "One final message—a message that is too often forgotten by parents in the day-to-day struggle and frustration of raising a child with autism. There is hope."

All healthy children have great stores of energy, but hyperactive children rarely sit still, have trouble concentrating, and often act on impulse. This hyperactive boy is playing a dangerous game, leaping among slippery rocks high above the water.

5

ATTENTION-DEFICIT AND DISRUPTIVE BEHAVIOR DISORDERS

I n 1863, Heinrich Hoffman wrote a poem about a restless, fidgety boy who caused problems for his parents:

"Phil, stop acting like a worm,
The table is no place to squirm."
Thus speaks the father to the son,
Severely says it, not in fun.
Mother frowns and looks around,
Although she doesn't make a sound.
But Philipp will not take advice,
He'll have his way at any price.
He turns,
And churns,
He wiggles
And jiggles
Here and there on the chair;
"Phil, these twists I cannot bear."

It is possible that Philipp was just a fidgety child. But it is also possible that today Philipp would be diagnosed as having attention-deficit/hyperactivity disorder (ADHD).

Most of us know at least one child like Philipp. These youngsters are usually considered the Dennis the Menaces of the world, children who are constantly into mischief, who can't sit still, who learned to run before they ever learned to walk. In the world of Winnie the Pooh, Tigger would be the one with ADHD, bouncing through life before he thinks through the consequences of his actions.

WHAT IS ADHD?

The *DSM-IV* defines ADHD as a condition characterized by a persistent pattern of inattention and of activity and impulsivity. The symptoms usually appear before the age of seven. In fact, parents of children with ADHD often say that, when they look back, they can identify these behaviors from the child's toddlerhood. Even so, toddlers are rarely diagnosed with ADHD, since many children who appear hyperactive and inattentive at this stage eventually outgrow these behaviors. In addition, in order for a diagnosis of ADHD to be made, there must be clear evidence that the impulsive and hyperactive behaviors are interfering with the child's age-appropriate functioning at a social, academic, or occupational level.

In his book *Attention-Deficit Hyperactivity Disorder*, Dr. Russell A. Barkley describes a five-year-old ADHD patient named Keith. In the doctor's waiting room, Keith hopped from chair to chair, swung his arms and legs, and fiddled with the light switches. All the while, he never stopped talking. At one point, he broke into a game that some other children were playing. When the children complained about Keith's rudeness and moved away, he didn't seem to know what to do with the

SIGNS OF ADHD

SIGNS OF INATTENTION

- being easily distracted by irrelevant sights and sounds
- failing to follow instructions carefully and completely
- failing to pay attention to details and making careless mistakes
- losing or forgetting objects, such as toys, pencils, and books

SIGNS OF HYPERACTIVITY AND IMPULSIVITY

- blurting out answers without listening fully to the questions
- experiencing difficulty waiting in line or taking turns
- running, climbing, or getting up from a seat when quiet behavior is expected
- squirming or fidgeting with hands or feet

toys that had been left to him. He seemed unable to entertain himself quietly.

Dr. Barkley looks at ADHD in terms of two sets of symptoms: inattention and a combination of hyperactive and impulsive behaviors. "Most children are more active, distractible, and impulsive than adults," he acknowledges. "And they are more inconsistent, affected by momentary events and dominated by objects in their immediate environment. The younger the children, the less able they are to be aware of time or to give priority to future events over more immediate wants. Such behaviors are signs of problems, however, when children display them significantly more than their peers do."

According to the *American Psychiatric Press Textbook of Psychiatry*, about 6 percent of all school-aged children suffer from ADHD. Dr. Barkley points out that boys are at least three times as likely as girls to develop the disorder. Boys may even outnumber girls with these symptoms by as much as nine to one. In addition, ADHD often appears in combination with other disorders. This means that children like Philipp and Keith are likely to have other problems besides fidgeting.

CAUSES OF ADHD

For years researchers thought that ADHD resulted from an inability in the brain to filter out competing inputs. In other words, they believed that neurological impairment caused a child with this problem to experience constant distraction by sights and sounds. However, Peter Szatmari's essay "The Epidemiology of Attention-Deficit Hyperactivity Disorder" reports that recent research paints a different picture. It indicates that ADHD is not so much a disorder of attention as it is a developmental failure in the brain circuitry that underlies inhibition and self-control. In other words, children with ADHD can't control their responses to sensory input. Dr. Barkley notes, in addition, that researchers have found children with ADHD to be less capable of thinking ahead, of preparing their actions in anticipation of upcoming events, than are other youngsters. And even when they have received feedback that they are making mistakes in the performance of a specific task, they typically fail to slow down to improve accuracy.

Scientists are still uncertain of the exact neurological causes for these behaviors. However, Dr. Barkley cites research that indicates that certain parts of the brain, the sections that regulate attention, are smaller in people who have ADHD. Although it is unknown why these neurological structures shrink in individuals with this condition, Szatmari suggests that mutations in several genes may play a role.

The most conclusive evidence that genetics contribute to the development of ADHD comes from studies of twins. Research by J. J. Gillis and colleagues indicates that when one identical twin has ADHD, the other identical twin has up to a 92 percent chance of developing the disorder. A study of twins by H. Gjone, J. Stevenson, and J. M. Sundet, reported in *Behavior Genetics*, found ADHD to have a heritability of close to 80 percent. This indicates that up to 80 percent of the differences in attention, hyperactivity, and impulsivity between people who have and people who don't have ADHD can be explained by genetic factors.

Research by G. J. LaHoste and colleagues, reported in the journal *Molecular Psychiatry*, suggests that the defective genes are the ones that tell dopamine, a chemical in the brain, how to carry messages from one nerve cell to another. Thus, children with this genetic defect have less control over their own behavior.

Doctors once believed that ADHD was caused by excessive sugar consumption or by poor child-rearing methods. But, to date, no research has been found to support this speculation. According to Dr. Barkley, however, some nongenetic causes have been linked to ADHD. These include premature birth, alcohol and tobacco use during pregnancy, exposure to high levels of lead during early childhood, and brain injuries. Together, these factors may explain 20 to 30 percent of ADHD cases among boys and a smaller percentage of cases among girls. Most cases of ADHD, in other words, are linked to genetic inheritance.

THE DIAGNOSIS AND TREATMENT OF ADHD

Many parents see signs of ADHD long before their child enters school. For example, as a preschooler, Philipp (the boy in Hoffman's poem) was probably unable to attend to a simple game or sit still long enough to hear a story read to him. He probably darted from activity to activity, driving his parents and older siblings to distraction.

In many cases, however, family members dismiss this sort of behavior as normal toddler energy. But once Philipp starts school, his teacher may notice that he has difficulty staying seated and paying attention to instructions. Because teachers work with many children in the same age group, they can often determine more easily than parents can that a child's behavior is different from that of other youngsters that age. As a result, Philipp's teacher may be the person who refers him to another professional for evaluation.

Various professionals, including school psychologists, psychiatrists, pediatricians, family doctors, and neurologists can make the diagnosis of ADHD. The first task in the evaluation process is to rule out other explanations for the behavior, such as emotional disorders, minor seizures, and poor vision or hearing. A doctor may also look at nutritional factors that can cause hyperactivity in a child (for instance, excessive consumption of caffeine). The professional will observe the youngster's behavior and gather information from the child's teachers (past and current) and from family members to determine how the youngster reacts to different situations and environments.

An accurate diagnosis is an important part of the treatment of ADHD. Only then can a combination of emotional, medical, and educational help allow the child to move ahead in his or her life. The two main types of treatment for this disorder are medication and *psychosocial intervention* (a treatment that addresses the emotions of the individual as well as his or her family or other social environment).

MEDICATIONS THAT TREAT ADHD

According to Dr. Barkley, 70 to 80 percent of all children with ADHD respond positively to *psychostimulants* (medications that affect a person's emotional state by stimulating increased neurochemical functioning). These medications can decrease impulsivity and hyperactivity; increase attention; and, in some children, decrease aggression. The most commonly used psychostimulants for ADHD are Ritalin (methylphenidate), Dexedrine (dextroamphetamine), and Cylert (pemoline). Side effects of these drugs include loss of appetite, loss of weight, and difficulty sleeping. Often however, these effects can be managed by adjusting the dosage of the medication. Regular monitoring of the different levels of medication is important to ensure proper dosage.

When psychostimulants prove to be ineffective or cause unacceptable side effects, *antidepressants* (medications that work to clinically prevent feelings of depression) have been found to be effective for some children

Methylphenidate is a neural stimulant that has become the most widely used medication in the treatment of attention-deficit disorder and hyperactivity. The number of prescriptions dispensed for the drug—shown here under its trade name, Ritalin—increased 260 percent from 1992 to 1997.

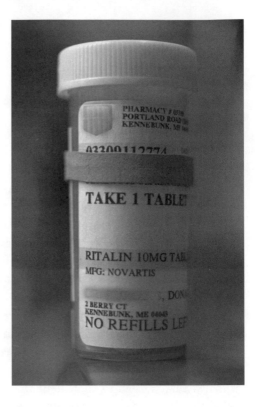

with ADHD. Like psychostimulants, these drugs can help the child compensate for the neurological abnormality that results in impulsive and hyperactive behavior.

OTHER TREATMENTS

The most important nonmedication treatment for children with ADHD usually takes place in the classroom. Because federal laws guarantee children with ADHD and other disorders an "appropriate" education, school psychologists and special education teachers must help develop an IEP (see chapter 3) to meet the educational needs of each child. In the case of a child with ADHD, the IEP will include activities that help the youngster monitor and control his or her own attention and behavior.

Other psychosocial treatments are sometimes effective as well. Psychotherapy, or counseling, can help children with ADHD to improve their self-esteem. Behavior modification techniques can help them change actual behaviors. Social skills training can teach youngsters with ADHD new behaviors by allowing them to practice skills such as sharing, taking turns, and interpreting the facial expressions and tones of voice of others. Support groups can show children with ADHD and their parents that they are not alone. Training in parenting skills can give parents the necessary tools—such as "time out" and behavior modification techniques—to manage their children's behavior. Stress management techniques can help parents and children deal with their frustrations more effectively.

Because children with ADHD cannot regulate their own emotions or behavior easily, it is important that their environments, both at home and at school, be structured. Children with ADHD need reliable, consistent reinforcement for appropriate behavior. Reinforcement must be frequent and intense. (In other words, where the promise of a weekly sticker might motivate the average child to complete school tasks, children with ADHD tend to need larger and more frequent sources of motivation.) Long-term tasks should be broken down into smaller, more manageable steps.

Federal law requires that schools provide education to all children with attention-deficit disorder, turning schools into important treatment centers. Here a special education program helps ADD children control their behavior and increase their attention spans.

Some families resist the use of drugs. This boy was diagnosed with attention-deficit disorder, but his mother, seen in the background, filed a civil rights complaint with the U.S. Department of Education charging that the staff of his school was pressuring her to give him Ritalin.

Many children will not outgrow ADHD. There is no cure for the disorder. However, people with this condition can learn to adapt to it and can live happy, productive, fulfilling lives. The organization CHADD (Children and Adults with Attention-Deficit/Hyperactivity Disorder) stresses that all people with ADHD have many talents and abilities that they can use to enhance their lives. According to CHADD:

> Many people with ADHD even feel that their patterns of behavior give them unique, often unrecognized, advantages. People with ADHD tend to be outgoing and ready for action. Because of their drive for excitement and stimulation, many become successful in business, sports, construction, and public speaking. Because of their ability to think about many things at once, many have won acclaim as artists and inventors.

MYTHS ABOUT PSYCHOSTIMULANT MEDICATIONS

Myth: The use of psychostimulants can lead to drug addiction later in life.

Fact: Since these drugs help many children succeed better in school, at home, and at play, they can help improve a child's sense of self-esteem and thus perhaps even prevent future drug abuse.

Myth: If a person responds well to psychostimulants, it means that he or she has ADHD.

Fact: These medications can help even people who don't have ADHD to focus their attention. However, improvement is generally more noticeable in people with ADHD.

Myth: Use of medication for attention deficit and disruptive behavior disorders should be stopped when a child reaches adolescence.

Fact: About 80 percent of individuals with these conditions who need medication as children need it as teenagers as well, and 50 percent continue to need medication as adults.

Myth: Medication will cause children to be "foggy" and act dull.

Fact: Children with ADHD who take psychostimulants usually seem more alert, since they are better able to focus and pay attention.

Myth: Psychostimulants have dangerous side effects.

Fact: Research indicates that these drugs are safe. The body excretes psychostimulants quickly. When side effects do occur, they are mild, do not threaten a child's well-being, and can often be eliminated or diminished by adjusting dosages.

Adapted from the National Institute of Mental Health's "Attention Deficit Hyperactivity Disorder." NIH Publication No. 96-3572, 1996.

As with every disorder, a positive attitude is a vital component to successful treatment. People with ADHD face many challenges, but they all have the potential to enrich our world.

OTHER DISRUPTIVE BEHAVIOR DISORDERS

The *DSM-IV* lists two additional disruptive behavior disorders: conduct disorder and oppositional defiant disorder. These conditions can often, but do not always, occur along with ADHD. According to Dr. Barkley, at least one-half of all children diagnosed with ADHD also have conduct or oppositional defiant disorders. And frequently when children with ADHD do not receive proper treatment, both at home and at school, symptoms of an additional disruptive behavior disorder eventually develop. According to the *American Psychiatric Press Textbook of Psychiatry*, many children with disruptive behavior disorders develop antisocial personality disorder in adulthood (a condition characterized by lack of regard for, and violation of, the rights of others). In fact, 85 percent of all youths in prison suffer from a disruptive behavior disorder.

CONDUCT DISORDER

The *DSM-IV* defines conduct disorder as a "repetitive and persistent behavior in which the basic rights of others or major age-appropriate social norms or rules are violated." M. Zoccolillo's article "Gender and the Development of Conduct Disorder" estimates that between 2 and 6 percent of all school-aged children are diagnosed with this disorder. The rate of conduct disorder among boys is approximately three to four times the rate among girls, with incidence increasing in adolescence.

Alan E. Kazdin's essay "Conduct Disorder" relates the case of a seven-year-old boy named Shawn who was referred for treatment because of his aggression toward his younger sisters at home and his peers at school. Shawn constantly argued with family members, threw tantrums, and occasionally stole from his stepfather. Shawn's teachers were unable to control his behavior. He fought with his schoolmates, argued with his teachers, and continually disrupted class.

Dr. Kazdin's treatment for Shawn involved parent management training. For two years a clinician worked with Shawn's mother to teach her effective behaviors toward Shawn and her other children. In particular, the clinician taught Shawn's mother to work with concrete behav-

Conduct disorder is diagnosed three to four times more frequently in boys than in girls. Adolescents with this disorder will frequently fight with their peers or argue with teachers. Here two young men are restrained by their friends before a bad situation gets worse.

WARNING SIGNS OF CONDUCT DISORDER

When onset of symptoms occurs before age 18, the following behaviors can be considered to be warning signs of conduct disorder:

1. failure to conform to social norms, such as impulsivity, lack of remorse, or truancy or running away;
2. lying;
3. violence toward people or property, such as assault, cruelty to people or animals, fire setting, forced sexual activity, robbery, or vandalism.

iors instead of simply reacting to a general, overall feeling of frustration. Shawn's mother also learned to reinforce positive behaviors with praise and tangible rewards and to discourage negative behaviors with mild punishment. Teachers followed through with the same behavior modification program at school.

After about five months, Shawn's behavior began to show improvement. He no longer argued as much with his family, friends, or teachers. Shawn's parents felt much more capable of managing his behavior. Although he continued to have occasional heated arguments with other children on the playground, he showed less physical aggression than he had exhibited before treatment.

OPPOSITIONAL DEFIANT DISORDER

Children with oppositional defiant disorder tend to "talk back" to and disobey people in authority. Unlike children with conduct disorder, however, these youngsters respect the personal rights of others. According to the *DSM-IV*, a diagnosis of oppositional defiant disorder requires that a child show "a recurrent pattern of negativistic, defiant, disobedient, and hostile behavior toward authority figures that persists for at least 6 months." In addition, the child frequently engages in at least four of the following behaviors:

- actively defying or refusing to comply with the requests or rules of adults
- arguing with authority figures
- blaming others for his or her own mistakes or misbehavior
- deliberately engaging in behaviors that annoy other people
- exhibiting spitefulness or vindictiveness
- losing his or her temper

All children behave in these ways at one time or another, but as with other conditions, diagnosis as a disorder is a question of degree. To qualify as an oppositional defiant disorder, the behaviors must occur more frequently than they do in most children of the same age or developmental level. The conduct must also lead to significant impairment in social, academic, or occupational functioning. In other words, the young person with oppositional defiant disorder will find that the behaviors cause frequent problems with family, with friends, at school, and (where applicable) at work.

According to the *DSM-IV*, between 2 and 16 percent of all children have oppositional defiant disorder. The condition is more common among boys than among girls, and the number of symptoms increases with age. Typically, the disorder becomes evident before age eight, and the onset is gradual, usually occurring over months or even years. The *DSM-IV* indicates that many children who start out with this disorder eventually develop the more serious condition of conduct disorder.

The *American Psychiatric Press Textbook of Psychiatry* notes that children with oppositional defiant disorder tend to have poor self-esteem. They are typically angry and frustrated with their world, particularly with the authority figures who seek to regulate their behavior. The fights that these youngsters engage in are often self-defeating. They would rather lose just about anything (a privilege or a toy, for example) other than the struggle.

Researchers such as David P. Farrington (in the *Journal of Child Psychiatry*); Rolf Loeber (in the *Clinical Psychology Review*); and Gerald R. Patterson, John B. Reid, and Thomas J. Dishion (in *Antisocial Boys*) note that defiant behavior can be the result of harsh, unstructured, and chaotic home environments. In *Defiant Children*, Dr. Barkley indicates that the cause of defiant behaviors is sometimes a combination of family environment, neurological functioning, and genetic heredity.

Tourette syndrome nearly ended the career of ballplayer Jim Eisenreich, forcing him onto the disabled list and then into retirement. With the right diagnosis and treatment, however, Eisenreich worked his way back to the major leagues. He became an excellent hitter and fielder and played in two World Series.

6

TIC DISORDERS

Kathy Clark was an average, happy baby who grew into an average, happy child. But when she was seven years old, her parents noticed that she was developing several nervous habits. She constantly shrugged her shoulders, and at the same time she would give her neck a little jerk as though she had a crick in it. She also blinked a lot. And she sniffed frequently and cleared her throat over and over again. Kathy's parents tried to ignore these behaviors. If these were nervous habits, they reasoned, they didn't want to make Kathy more nervous by calling attention to what were probably just harmless little mannerisms. Besides, the few times that they had mentioned the behaviors, Kathy seemed unable to stop herself from performing them.

Then Kathy's arms began jerking, as though she were a puppet on a string. Her parents were beginning to feel frightened now, and so was Kathy. She simply couldn't keep these behaviors from occurring.

Suddenly, when Kathy was 10, all of her nervous habits disappeared. Her parents heaved a sigh of relief—until Kathy abruptly began hooting and barking. Just as she had been unable to stop herself from twitching and jerking, now she could not keep from making loud, bizarre sounds over and over again until her throat ached. At last the Clarks sought help from a doctor who was both a psychiatrist and a neurologist. She told them that Kathy had a neurological disorder known as Tourette syndrome, a type of *tic disorder*.

WHAT ARE TICS?

Tics are brief behaviors that, although they may resemble some purposeful act, serve no purpose and are repeated over and over. They can be muscular, such as Kathy's jerking and blinking, or they can be vocal, such as Kathy's hooting and barking. They can be simple twitches or grunts, or they can be more complex, involving bending, grimacing, and echoing the words of others. Some tics involve uncontrollable outbursts of profanity or obscenity.

Tics are brief, involuntary behaviors that serve no purpose and are repeated over and over. Some may be as simple as a twitching in the face, of the sort shown here. Others may be much more complex and disruptive.

Others are so complex that they meet the criteria for *obsessive-compulsive disorder*—a condition characterized by recurrent obsessions (persistent thoughts or ideas) or compulsions (repetitive, ritualistic behaviors) that are time-consuming and distressful and that significantly impair a person's life.

Tic behaviors, whether simple or complex, are involuntary. Sometimes they can be consciously suppressed, but only temporarily. If Kathy tries not to hoot or jerk, for example, she will begin to feel more and more tense—until eventually the tic bursts out. Ultimately, Kathy cannot keep this from happening.

In addition to Tourette syndrome, the *DSM-IV* lists two other tic disorders: transient tic and chronic tic. Transient tic is characterized by episodes of tic behavior that can last from two weeks to a year. Chronic tic persists for more than a year and involves either muscular *or* vocal tics. Tourette syndrome involves both muscular *and* vocal tics, with symptoms that endure for more than a year, usually throughout life. All

Table 2
Examples of Tic Behaviors

Muscular Tics		Vocal Tics	
Simple	*Complex*	*Simple*	*Complex*
blinking	making faces	coughing	swearing
jerking	touching hair	clearing throat	echoing
shrugging	jumping	grunting	repeating
grimacing	touching objects	snorting	
	hitting oneself	sniffing	

of the tic disorders are typically diagnosed before 18 years of age. Their onset is usually between ages 2 and 13. According to *American Psychiatric Press Textbook of Psychiatry*, 1 to 2 percent of all people have some form of tic disorder, and about 1 in 1,500 individuals has Tourette syndrome (TS). According to the Tourette Syndrome Association, "The official estimate by the National Institutes of Health is that 100,000 Americans have full-blown TS." As many as 12 percent of all children show some form of tic symptoms, however. Tic behaviors tend to worsen during puberty and adolescence and become less severe later in life.

The frequency of the tic behavior generally waxes and wanes throughout a person's lifetime. Symptoms may suddenly seem to disappear (as they did with Kathy) and then just as suddenly, for no apparent reason, reappear at a new level of intensity or in a new form. Concentrating on a task can, but does not always, help to suppress tics temporarily. In general, tics are unpredictable. They vary from person to person, from day to day, and from year to year.

CAUSES OF TIC DISORDERS

Tic behaviors can look so bizarre that people with this disorder were once thought to be insane or possessed by demons. Although tics may occur more frequently when a person is upset or tense, however, the disorder itself is neurological rather than psychological. In other words, tic behaviors are caused by a chemical abnormality in the brain rather than by an emotional problem.

According to researchers Ben J. M. Van de Wetering and P. Heutink (authors of the book *The Genetics of the Gilles de la Tourette Syndrome*),

Because they are subject to fits of behavior others see as bizarre, children with tic disorders may be ridiculed or rejected by their peers—or even by adults, who should know better. This young girl endures the taunting of her classmates.

most of the current research indicates that, although some cases of tic disorders seem to have been triggered by a trauma to the brain, the condition is generally inherited genetically. Georges Gilles de la Tourette, who first studied people with tic disorders in the late 19th century, recognized that the disorder seemed to have a genetic basis. However, scientists did not follow up on his research until nearly a century later. Consequently, until the 1970s most doctors believed tic disorders to be a psychological problem.

As a result, many worried parents received the blame for their children's condition. They were told that "poor parenting techniques" caused their children to "act out" their frustration through verbal and motor tics. Then, in the mid-1960s, scientists began to look at data that indicated a biological, rather than a psychological, cause for tics. In 1978, when Dr. Arthur Shapiro and colleagues published the results of their research in the book *Gilles de la Tourette Syndrome*, the medical world finally became convinced that tic disorders were not a symptom of mental illness.

Scientists have not yet identified the brain abnormality that causes tics, but they have some clues. They know that *electroencephalograms* (EEGs)—recordings taken by a machine that traces brain waves—of at least half of all individuals with Tourette syndrome show an abnormal pattern. In other words, the EEGs indicate that the brain activity of people with this disorder is somehow different from that of individuals without the condition. In his essay "Tic Disorders," Irwin J. Mansdorf indicates that tic disorders may be caused by abnormalities in the metabolism of dopamine, a chemical that carries messages in the brain.

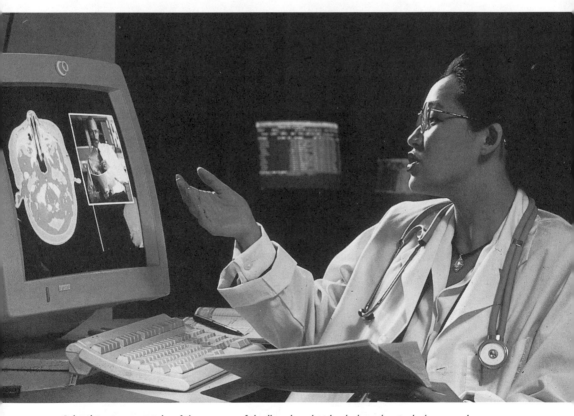

Scientists are uncertain of the causes of tic disorders, but brain imaging techniques such as electroencephalograms and magnetic resonance imaging, shown here, are providing important clues. One researcher suggests that tic disorders may be caused by chemical imbalances in the brain.

COMPLEX VOCAL AND MOTOR TICS

The following complex vocal and motor tics can cause serious problems at school, at work, and in public places:

Coprolalia are outbursts of obscene, profane, or other socially unacceptable words or phrases. Shimberg's *Living with Tourette Syndrome* estimates that only about 10 to 30 percent of all people who have Tourette syndrome experience this disturbing symptom. However, the *American Psychiatric Press Textbook of Psychiatry* estimates that the symptom occurs in 60 percent of all people with this syndrome. According to Shimberg, those who experience coprolalia may find themselves "quietly walking down the street or engaging in normal conversation, then suddenly muttering or shouting an unacceptable word or phrase, which may include ethnic or religious slurs or references to anatomy, sexual acts, bodily functions, and other derogatory words or phrases. The utterance seldom reflects the thoughts or opinions of the person saying them."

Corpropraxia is the performance of obscene or socially unacceptable actions, such as "giving the finger" or pointing at and grabbing one's own or someone else's genitals.

Echolalia is the repetition of another person's last word, phrase, or sentence. Occasionally, someone with this condition may repeat a sound, such as a dog's bark or a cat's meow.

Echopraxia is the imitation of the gestures and movements of others. This can cause other people to believe that they are being mocked.

Palilalia is the repetition of the person's own last word, phrase, or sound, making the individual sound like a broken record.

Tic disorders frequently appear within the same family. Often a parent and a child or two or more siblings share the condition. According to the Tourette Syndrome Association, the genetic tendency to Tourette syndrome is transmitted from the parent to the child. This means that if one parent carries the gene for tic syndrome, each child has about a

50 percent chance of inheriting the genetic tendency for the disorder. Not all children who inherit this predisposition will display symptoms, however.

The Tourette Syndrome Association estimates that a girl who inherits the genetic tendency for the condition has about a 70 percent chance of developing some form of tic disorder. But a boy who inherits the tendency has about a 99 percent chance of developing some form of the disorder. The condition is far more common among boys than among girls. According to Elaine Fantle Shimberg's *Living with Tourette Syndrome*, however, only about 10 percent of children who inherit the gene for tic disorders will ever experience symptoms severe enough to require medical attention. Most people, Shimberg stresses, "have such mild symptoms that they never become patients and are never diagnosed by health-care professionals." They can, however, carry the gene to the next generation.

TREATMENT OF TIC DISORDERS

Health care professionals have various approaches to the treatment of tic disorders. Because a tic is a concrete, observable behavior, some experts recommend using a behavior modification approach to keep tics under control. Others believe that counseling, relaxation training, and family therapy can best help people with this disorder to modify the situations and environments that trigger tics. Still other professionals, however, consider medication to be the answer.

In their groundbreaking work *Gilles de la Tourette Syndrome*, Dr. Shapiro and colleagues wrote, "Everything works with Tourette Syndrome . . . for a while." What this means is that, because tic behaviors wax and wane, doctors may be convinced that they have hit upon the perfect treatment—only to have a new tic behavior emerge in full force.

Many parents are uncomfortable with having their children medicated to control their tics. They are often concerned about side effects. However, dosage control can sometimes take care of this problem. In his book *The Man Who Mistook His Wife for a Hat*, Dr. Oliver Sacks tells the story of Ray, a young amateur drummer who had Tourette syndrome.

When Ray took his medication, he became "musically 'dull,' average, competent, but lacking energy, enthusiasm, extravagance, and joy. He no longer had his tics or compulsive hitting of the drums—but he also no longer had wild and creative surges." However, Ray and his doctor eventually made the compromise that Ray would take his medication during his day job and go without it on weekends when he played his music. This allowed him to be "witty ticcy Ray" when it was more appropriate for him to be so. As this case indicates, sensitivity to individual needs is an important aspect of the treatment of tic disorders.

Because many children with tic disorders have other conditions as well (such as attention-deficit/hyperactivity disorder or Asperger's disorder), medication is sometimes prescribed to alleviate these associated problems. It is important to keep in mind that, when we talk about Tourette syndrome or other tic disorders, we are not talking about diseases. We are talking about a collection of symptoms that occur together. Each individual's symptoms are unique, and each treatment plan must be unique as well.

According to Shimberg, 70 percent or more of the people who have Tourette syndrome have only mild tics. These individuals, she stresses, "do not require any type of treatment, medical or otherwise, to help them deal with their symptoms. For these people, [Tourette syndrome] is a minor inconvenience, an occasional source of embarrassment, nothing more."

As we have seen with other disorders, one of the most important factors in successful treatment disorders is a positive outlook. In their article "Neuropsychiatric Disorders of Childhood," Donald J. Cohen and James F. Leckman state:

> The individuals with [Tourette syndrome] who do the best, we believe, are: those who have been able to feel relatively good about themselves and remain close to their families; those who have the capacity for humor and friendship; those who are less burdened by troubles with attention and behavior, particularly aggression; and those who have not had development derailed by medication. Children with . . . quite severe tics may develop into outgoing, happily married and successful young adults.

Leckman and Cohen expand on this viewpoint in their book *Tourette's Syndrome*:

> One of the pleasures of a long involvement with children with Tourette's syndrome has been to see that this optimistic attitude is quite often empirically valid. Indeed, most children with Tourette's syndrome, even those with the most severe difficulties in the school-age years, develop into functioning and competent adults. Often they are free from tics, or virtually free of them, unless under stress. Their tics become less noticeable as they are no longer under

the microscopic scrutiny of parents and other adults who often see a child's imperfections under a high degree of magnification.

Many support groups exist for people with Tourette syndrome and for parents of children with tic disorders. These groups generally stress that tic disorders do not have to be perceived in a negative way. Tic disorders may be lifelong conditions, but they are not fatal. Moreover, these organizations point out, people with tic disorders tend to have a quirky creativity, humorous energy. "Ticcers" look at the world from a unique perspective that enriches the lives of those around them.

One adult with Tourette syndrome recommends the following when dealing with children who have this disorder: "The biggest thing you can do is just treat them like a normal kid. And if you do that, they'll feel like a normal kid. But if you treat them like it's horrible and they have some disease, that's how they'll feel."

Some developmental disorders may be seen in very young children, such as this one. These disorders include feeding problems, excessive anxiety, and problems in urinating.

7

OTHER DISORDERS
DIAGNOSED
IN CHILDHOOD

llen and Lisa Brown are young parents with a two-year-old daughter named Jessica. Jessica seems to be physically healthy, but her parents have noticed that her behavior is sometimes different from that of the other children in her day care group. She says only a few words, she has not yet begun to use the potty, and she is still a little unsteady on her feet. Allen's mother insists that Allen and his siblings passed these developmental milestones much more quickly than Jessica. She also points out that Jessica likes only a few foods and that she often cries when she is separated from Lisa. Jessica's other grandmother believes that Jessica is not as bright as her other grandchildren. Although Allen and Lisa resent their mothers' interference, their concerns have prompted them to do some reading about childhood problems. What they have learned has not put their worries to rest. In fact, they are beginning to fear that Jessica may have some sort of disorder.

In fact, Jessica is a perfectly normal little girl. All children develop at their own speed and in their own time. When we read about childhood disorders, many of us will recognize certain behaviors that seem characteristic of a child we know. However, parents (and other family members and friends) should never attempt to diagnose these problems themselves. Many individuals who show some of the symptoms associated with childhood disorders still function within the normal range. Only trained professionals can accurately diagnose and treat these conditions.

As always, however, when a disorder does exist, early diagnosis is important to effective treatment. If parents suspect that their child's behaviors indicate a problem, they should seek professional help.

The *DSM-IV* lists the following three additional categories of childhood disorders:

- feeding and eating disorders

- elimination disorders

- other disorders of infancy, childhood, or adolescence (including separation anxiety, selective mutism, reactive attachment disorder, and stereotypic movement)

FEEDING AND EATING DISORDERS

Three common feeding and eating disorders are pica, rumination disorder, and feeding disorder of infancy and early childhood.

PICA

The *DSM-IV* defines pica as the "persistent eating of nonnutritive substances for a period of at least 1 month." Pica is a condition that is common among, but not exclusive to, mentally retarded children. Babies with this disorder may eat paint, plaster, string, hair, or cloth. Older children may ingest sand, leaves, pebbles, insects, or even animal

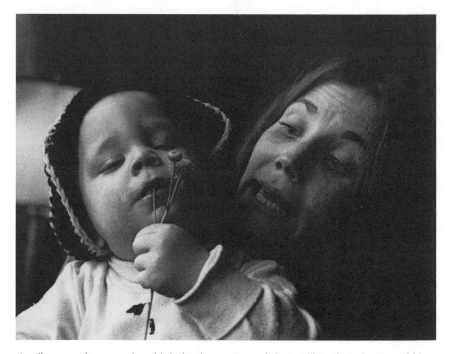

As all parents know, and as this baby demonstrates, infants will put just about anything in their mouths. A child who persistently consumes nonnutritive substances for more than one month, however, may have the eating disorder known as pica.

Children with rumination disorder spit up their food, but with no apparent nausea or retching. Up to 25 percent of children with this disorder die of malnutrition. This boy is unable to digest even a crust of bread.

droppings. We know that all toddlers put things in their mouth. According to the *DSM-IV*, this behavior must be inappropriate for the developmental level or age of the child for a diagnosis of pica to apply.

RUMINATION DISORDER

Children with rumination disorder repeatedly bring back into their mouths food that they have already eaten. They do so without any apparent nausea, retching, or feelings of disgust. Then they either spit it out or chew it and swallow it. The *DSM-IV* specifies that this behavior must occur for at least one month before the disorder can be diagnosed. This is a serious condition that should be reported immediately to a physician. Children with this disorder typically lose weight, and as many as 25 percent of all children with this problem die from malnutrition.

FEEDING DISORDER OF INFANCY OR EARLY CHILDHOOD

The *DSM-IV* defines feeding disorder of infancy or early childhood as the persistent failure of a child who is younger than six years old and who is offered sufficient food to eat adequately. The problem must persist for at least one month. As with rumination disorder, children who suffer from this problem typically lose weight or fail to gain sufficient weight as they grow. Many youngsters experience eating problems at one time or another. However, when this condition persists for a month or more, a physician should be consulted. The malnutrition that can result from this disorder sometimes leads to other health problems, such as anemia (a shortage of red blood cells) and nutrient deficiencies. In severe cases, the condition can even be life threatening.

ELIMINATION DISORDERS

Elimination is the discharge of body waste, and disorders in this area, though rarely life-threatening, can lead to great embarassment for older children. Two common types of elimination disorders are enuresis and encoprosis.

ENURESIS

The *DSM-IV* defines *enuresis* as "repeated voiding of urine during the day or at night into bed or clothes." This behavior is most often, but not always, involuntary. To qualify for a diagnosis of enuresis, a child must wet him- or herself at least twice a week for at least three months and must be at least five years old or have a mental age of at least five years. For a diagnosis of enuresis to apply, the condition cannot be caused by medication or by an underlying health problem.

According to the *DSM-IV*, enuresis occurs in about 7 percent of all boys and 3 percent of all girls at age 5. By age 10, the prevalence decreases to 3 percent for boys and 2 percent for girls. By age 18, the condition is found in only about 1 percent of all boys and under 1 percent of girls.

Since there is such a steady rate of "spontaneous remission" of enuresis—that is, almost all children naturally outgrow this condition—authors such as Eugene C. Walker wonder whether there is a real need to treat enuresis at all. In his essay "Elimination Disorders," Walker indicates that treatment should depend on each child's family and social situation. He suggests that if the bed-wetting causes family conflict and tension, or if the child is embarrassed or teased by other children because of the condition, then treatment is probably needed.

The most effective method of treatment, claims Walker, is the pad-and-bell treatment. This involves a moisture-sensitive pad that rings an alarm and wakes the child when the pad gets wet. Walker cites several research studies that indicate that after 8 to 12 weeks of use, 75 to 90 percent of all children who use the pad-and-bell treatment no longer wet the bed. These devices are available in many stores, but they are most effective when used under the supervision of a physician or therapist.

Other treatments for enuresis include medication, hypnosis, and sphincter muscle exercises. These approaches have varying degrees of success from individual to individual. In the end, however, most children simply outgrow the condition.

ENCOPRESIS

The main characteristic of *encopresis* is the repeated passage of feces in inappropriate places (for example, in the clothing or on the floor). As with enuresis, this behavior is usually, but not always, involuntary. Walker estimates that between 1.5 and 7.5 percent of all children experience encopresis at some point in their childhood. Boys are four to five times more likely than girls to develop the condition.

Many children experience the symptoms of encopresis at one time or another. In order to be considered a disorder, according to the *DSM-IV*, the behavior must occur at least once a month for at least three months, and the child must have a developmental age equivalent to four years or more. (Children with mental retardation or autism, for instance, may not be toilet trained by age four because they have not yet reached a developmental age of four years. In this case, a diagnosis of encopresis would not apply.) For this behavior to be considered a disorder, according to the *DSM-IV*, it must not be caused by a medical condition.

The older a child is, the more embarrassing and upsetting this disorder is likely to be to him or her. Health care professionals should be consulted to rule out any underlying health problem. Counseling and behavior management programs can help parents and children gain control of this behavior. In almost all cases, however, children outgrow this condition on their own.

OTHER DISORDERS OF INFANCY, CHILDHOOD, OR ADOLESCENCE

Other miscellaneous disorders of childhood include separation anxiety disorder, selective mutism, reactive attachment disorder, and stereotypic movement disorder.

SEPARATION ANXIETY DISORDER

A child with separation anxiety disorder experiences an excessive degree of anxiety when away from home or separated from the person to whom he or she is most attached. The *DSM-IV* specifies that, in order for a diagnosis of separation anxiety disorder to apply, the disturbance must last for at least four weeks and must interfere with other areas of functioning, whether social or academic. A diagnosis of separation anxiety is not appropriate in cases in which the behavior is associated with a pervasive developmental disorder or a psychotic disorder. (A psychotic disorder is a condition characterized by delusions [false beliefs that a person maintains despite obvious evidence to the contrary], hallucinations [sensory perceptions, usually involving sight, hearing, or smell, of something that is not actually present], disorganized speech, and/or grossly disorganized or catatonic behavior [characterized by a complete lack of attention to surroundings].)

Children who have separation anxiety disorder are typically homesick and unhappy whenever they're away from home. A child with this condition who is separated from the person who is the focus of his or her attachment may repeatedly call the individual on the phone and ask questions about the person's whereabouts. These youngsters are often preoccupied with fears about accidents or sickness that might separate them permanently from their attachment figures. They are uncomfortable when they are away from home by themselves, and they sometimes refuse to attend school. They tend to be clingy, following their parents around the house because they are reluctant to let them out of their sight.

Youngsters with this condition may have difficulty falling asleep at night and may insist that someone stay with them at bedtime. Because their sleep is often disturbed by nightmares about catastrophes that disrupt the family, they frequently get up and make their way to their parents' beds.

Children sometimes develop this disorder after a traumatic event (such as the illness or death of a loved one) or after a major life change (such as a move to a new neighborhood or a change of schools). Onset may be as early as the preschool years or as late as adolescence. Typically there are periods when the symptoms diminish, only to flare up again at a later stage. The condition often persists for years. According to the *DSM-IV*, about 4 percent of all children experience this problem.

This disorder can interfere significantly with an individual's ability to function emotionally, socially, and academically. However, family and individual therapy have proved to be effective treatments.

SELECTIVE MUTISM

In the language of the *DSM-IV*, the essential feature of selective mutism is "the persistent failure to speak in specific social situations (e.g., school, with playmates) where speaking is expected, despite speaking in other situations." That is, children with this disorder are able to talk but, in certain situations or with certain people, refuse to talk.

In order for a diagnosis of selective mutism to apply, the disturbance must last at least one month (not counting the child's first month of school), and it must interfere with the individual's educational (or occupational) and social functioning. A diagnosis of selective mutism should not be made if the child has a communication disorder (see chapter 3), a pervasive developmental disorder (see chapter 4), or a psychotic disorder. Children with this condition often communicate through gestures and by nodding or shaking their heads. When they do talk in situations in which they are uncomfortable, they generally speak in a strange, monotone voice and use only short phrases or monosyllables. Selective mutism is a rare disorder. According to the *DSM-IV*, it is found in only 1 percent of all individuals seen in mental health settings.

If a child is exhibiting this behavior, both individual counseling for the youngster and family therapy are recommended.

REACTIVE ATTACHMENT DISORDER

Reactive attachment disorder is a rare condition that is usually seen in children who have been physically or emotionally abused. As a result of the abuse, the child is unable to make normal emotional attachments to others. Onset is before age five, but the disorder may last throughout the person's lifetime. Treatment involves individual and family therapy. In many cases, the child's improvement depends upon removal from the home.

STEREOTYPIC MOVEMENT DISORDER

The *DSM-IV* defines stereotypic movement disorder as "motor behavior that is repetitive, often seemingly driven, and nonfunctional." The following behaviors are typical in this condition:

- body rocking
- eye poking
- face touching
- hair fingering
- hand flapping
- head banging
- breath holding
- object biting

- self-biting
- self-hitting
- self-scratching
- inappropriate laughing
- teeth grinding
- thumb sucking
- whirling

The two most common behaviors are head banging and body rocking. Children apparently engage in these behaviors as a form of self-stimulation, either to soothe themselves or to release tension.

According to the *American Psychiatric Press Textbook of Psychiatry*, about 15 to 20 percent of all normal children exhibit this disorder at one time or another. The incidence is much higher in deaf and blind children and in children with mental retardation, pervasive developmental disorders, or psychotic disorders. Among individuals who are severely or profoundly mentally retarded, the incidence of this condition may be as high as 60 percent.

Head banging and body rocking can begin as early as 6 to 12 months of age. In normal children, however, these behaviors typically disappear by age 4. When the behavior does not pass by itself, treatment includes behavior modification techniques, medication, and helping the child develop alternatives to the self-stimulating behaviors.

CONCLUSION

When we look at disorders first diagnosed in childhood, it is important to keep in mind that these conditions are not diseases. Rather, each one is a collection of behaviors that seem to occur together. Although in some cases an underlying biological abnormality may cause the behaviors, scientists are often unclear as to the exact nature of the physiological cause. Even in these instances, however, the diagnosis of the disorder is a question of degree. The symptoms of these conditions exist on a continuum, a range of occurrence. All of us may experience many of these behaviors at one time or another, but they do not constitute a disorder unless they interfere with our normal, everyday functioning. And even then, as Dr. Barkley points out in his book *Attention-Deficit Hyperactivity Disorder*, symptoms may change from setting to setting and from person to person.

The accurate diagnosis of childhood disorders allows children who are experiencing problems to receive the treatment that will help them best grow and develop. With that help, they can each achieve their full and unique potential.

The Arc
(Formerly the Association for
Retarded Citizens of the United
States)
1010 Wayne Avenue, Suite 650
Silver Spring, MD 20910
(301) 565-3842
(800) 433-5255
http://www.thearc.org

Autism Society of America
7910 Woodmont Avenue, Suite 300
Bethesda, MD 20814–3015
(800) 3AUTISM
(301) 657-0881
http://www.autism-society.org

Children and Adults with Attention-Deficit/Hyperactivity Disorder (CHADD)
8181 Professional Place, Suite 201
Landover, MD 20785
(301) 306-7070
(800) 233-4050
http://www.chadd.org

ERIC Clearinghouse on Disabilities and Gifted Education
1920 Association Drive
Reston, VA 20191–1589
(800) 328-0272
http://ericec.org

Exceptional Children's Assistance Center
P.O. Box 16
Davidson, NC 28036
(704) 892-1321
(800) 962-6817
http://www.ecacparentcenter.org

The 5p-Society
(For parents of children with cri du
chat syndrome)
7108 Katella Avenue, No. 502
Stanton, CA 90680
(888) 970-0777
http://www.fivepminus.org

International Rett Syndrome Association
9121 Piscataway Road, Suite 2B
Clinton, MD 20735
(301) 856-3334
(800) 818-RETT
http://www.rettsyndrome.org

Learning Disabilities Association of America
4156 Library Road
Pittsburgh, PA 15234
(412) 341-1515
(888) 300-6710
http://www.ldanatl.org

National Autism Hotline/Autism Services Center
605 Ninth Street
Prichard Building
Huntington, WV 25701
(304) 525-8014

National Council on Stuttering
1200 W. Harrison Street, Suite 2010
Chicago, IL 60607
(312) 996-3132

National Down Syndrome Congress
7000 Peachtree-Dunwoody Road
Building 5, Suite 100
Atlanta, GA 30328–1662
(800) 232-NDSC (6372)
http://www.ndsccenter.org

National Down Syndrome Society
666 Broadway, Suite 810
New York, NY 10012
(800) 221-4602
http://www.ndss.org

National Fragile X Foundation
P.O. Box 190488
San Francisco, CA 94119
(510) 763-6030
(800) 688-8765
http://www.nfxf.org

National Information Center for Children and Youth with Disabilities (NICHCY)
P.O. Box 1492
Washington, DC 20013
(800) 695-0285
http://www.nichcy.org

National Organization for Rare Disorders (NORD)
P.O. Box 8923
New Fairfield, CT 06812
(203) 746-6518
(800) 999-NORD (6673)
http://www.rarediseases.org

Tourette Syndrome Association
42-40 Bell Boulevard
Bayside, NY 11361–2874
(718) 224-2999
E-mail: tourette@ix.netcom.com

APPENDIX

BIBLIOGRAPHY

American Psychiatric Association. *Diagnostic and Statistical Manual of Mental Disorders.* 4th ed. Washington, D.C.: American Psychiatric Association, 1994.

American Psychiatric Press. *American Psychiatric Press Textbook of Psychiatry.* 2nd ed. Washington, D.C.: American Psychiatric Press, 1994.

Attwood, Tony. *Asperger's Syndrome: A Guide for Parents and Professionals.* Philadelphia: Jessica Kinsley, 1999.

Barkley, Russell A. *Attention-Deficit Hyperactivity Disorder.* New York: Guilford, 1998.

———. *Defiant Children.* New York: Guilford, 1997.

Cohen, Donald J., and James F. Leckman. "Neuropsychiatric Disorders of Childhood: Tourette's Syndrome as a Model." *Acta Paediatrica Supplement* 422 (1997): 106–11.

Cook, E. H., et al. "Association of Attention Deficit Disorder and the Dopamine Transporter Gene." *American Journal of Human Genetics* 56 (1995): 993–98.

Farrington, D. P. "The Twelfth Jack Tizard Memorial Lecture. The Development of Offending and Antisocial Behavior from Childhood: Key Findings from the Cambridge Study in Delinquent Development." *Journal of Child Psychiatry* 360 (1995): 929–64.

Frith, Uta. *Autism: Explaining the Enigma.* Cambridge, Mass.: Basil Blackwell, 1989.

Garber, H. J., and E. R. Ritvo. "Magnetic Resonance Imaging of the Posterior Fossa in Autistic Adults." *American Journal of Psychiatry* 149 (1992): 245–47.

Gillis, J. J., et al. "Attention Deficit Disorder in Reading-Disabled Twins: Evidence for Genetic Etiology." *Journal of Abnormal Child Psychology* 20 (1992): 303–15.

Gjone, H., J. Stevenson, and J. M. Sundet. "Changes in Heritability Across Increasing Levels of Behavior Problems in Young Twins." *Behavior Genetics* 26 (1996): 419–26.

Kanner, Leo. "Autistic Disturbances of Affective Contact." *Nervous Child* 2 (1943): 217–50.

Kazdin, Alan E. "Conduct Disorder." In *The Practice of Child Therapy*, ed. Richard J. Morris and Thomas R. Kratochwill. Boston: Allyn and Bacon, 1998.

LaHoste, G. J., et al. "Dopamine D4 Receptor Gene Polymorphism Is Associated with Attention Deficit Hyperactivity Disorder." *Molecular Psychiatry* 1 (1996): 121–24.

Leckman, James F., and Donald J. Cohen. *Tourette's Syndrome: Tics, Obsessions, Compulsions: Developmental Psychopathology and Clinical Care.* New York: John Wiley and Sons, 1998.

Loeber, Rolf. "Development and Risk Factors of Juvenile Antisocial Behavior and Delinquency." *Clinical Psychology Review* 10 (1990): 1–41.

Mansdorf, Irwin J. "Tic Disorders." In *Handbook of Child Behavior Therapy in the Psychiatric Setting*, ed. Robert T. Ammerman and Michel Hersen. New York: John Wiley and Sons, 1995.

Maxmen, Jerrold S., and Nicholas G. Ward. *Essential Psychopathology and Its Treatment*, 2nd ed. New York: Norton, 1995.

Morris, Richard J., and Thomas R. Kratochwill, eds. *The Practice of Child Therapy.* Boston: Allyn and Bacon, 1998.

Moser, H. W., C. T. Ramey, and C. O. Leonard. "Mental Retardation." In *Principles and Practice of Medical Genetics*, ed. A. E. H. Emery and D. L. Rimoin. Edinburgh: Churchill-Livingstone, 1988.

National Institute of Mental Health. "Attention Deficit Hyperactivity Disorder." NIH Publication No. 96-3572, 1996.

Patterson, G. R., J. B. Reid, and T. J. Dishion. *Antisocial Boys.* Eugene, Ore.: Castalia, 1992.

Powers, Michael D. *Children with Autism.* Rockville, Md.: Woodbine, 1989.

Pueschel, Siegfried M., James C. Bernier, and Leslie E. Weidenman. *The Special Child: A Source Book for Parents.* Baltimore, Md.: Paul H. Brooks, 1988.

Reid, William H., and George U. Balis, with Beverly J. Sutton. *The Treatment of Psychiatric Disorders.* Bristol, Pa.: Brunner/Mazel, 1997.

Sacks, Oliver. *The Man Who Mistook His Wife for a Hat.* New York: Dutton, 1986.

Seltzer, M. M., and M. W. Krauss. "Aging Parents with Mentally Retarded Children: Family Risk Factors and Sources of Support." *American Journal of Mental Retardation* 94 (1989): 303–12.

Shapiro, Arthur K., et al. *Gilles de la Tourette Syndrome.* New York: Raven, 1978.

Shimberg, Elaine Fantle. *Living with Tourette Syndrome.* New York: Simon and Schuster, 1995.

Stone, Wendy, William E. MacLean Jr., and Kerry L. Hogan. "Autism and Mental Retardation." In *Handbook of Pediatric Psychology.* Ed. Michael C. Roberts. New York: Guilford Press, 1995.

Szatmari, Peter. "The Epidemiology of Attention-Deficit Hyperactivity Disorder." In *Child and Adolescent Psychiatric Clinics of North America,* vol. 1, ed. G. Weiss. New York: W. B. Saunders, 1992.

Tirosh, E., and J. Canby. "Autism with Hyperlexia: A Distinct Sydrome?" *American Journal on Mental Retardation* 98 (1993): 84–92.

Van de Wetering, Ben J. M., and P. Heutink. *The Genetics of the Gilles de la Tourette Syndrome: A Review.* New York: Mosby–Year Book, 1993.

Walker, Eugene C. "Elimination Disorders: Enuresis and Encopresis." In *Handbook of Pediatric Psychology,* ed. Michael C. Roberts. New York: Guilford, 1995.

Zoccolillo, M. "Gender and the Development of Conduct Disorder." *Development and Pathology* 5 (1993): 65–78.

APPENDIX

FURTHER READING

Bain, Lisa J. *A Parent's Guide to Attention Deficit Disorders.* New York: Dell, 1991.

Barkley, Russell A. *Taking Charge of ADHD: The Complete Authoritative Guide for Parents.* New York: Guilford, 1995.

Bruun, Ruth Dowling, and Bertel Bruun. *A Mind of Its Own: Tourette's Syndrome—A Story and a Guide.* New York: Oxford University Press, 1994.

Dwyer, K. *What Do You Mean I Have a Learning Disability?* New York: Walker, 1991.

Fisher, Gary, and Rhoda Cummings. *The School Survival Guide for Kids with LD.* Minneapolis, Minn.: Free Spirit, 1991.

———. *When Your Child Has LD: A Survival Guide for Parents.* Minneapolis, Minn.: Free Spirit, 1995.

Flannery, Raymond B. *Preventing Youth Violence.* New York: Continuum, 1999.

Fowler, M. C. *Maybe You Know My Kid: A Parent's Guide to Identifying, Understanding, and Helping Your Child with Attention-Deficit Hyperactivity Disorder.* New York: Birch Lane, 1990.

Frith, Uta, ed. *Autism and Asperger's Syndrome.* New York: Cambridge University Press, 1991.

Haerle, Tracy. *Children with Tourette's Syndrome.* Rockville, Md.: Woodbine House, 1992.

Hallowell, E., and J. Ratey. *Driven to Distraction.* New York: Pantheon, 1994.

Hirschmann, Jane R., and Lela Zaphiropoulous. *Preventing Childhood Eating Disorders.* Carlsbad, Calif.: Gurze, 1993.

Johnson, Dorothy D. *I Can't Sit Still: Educating and Affirming Inattentive and Hyperactive Children.* Santa Cruz, Calif.: ETR, 1992.

Katz, Mark. *On Playing a Poor Hand Well: Insights from the Lives of Those Who Have Overcome Childhood Risks and Adversities.* New York: Norton, 1997.

Kumin, Libby. *Communication Skills in Children with Down Syndrome.* Rockville, Md.: Woodbine, 1994.

Levin, Toby. *Rainbow of Hope: A Guide for the Special Needs Child.* North Miami Beach, Fla.: Starlight Publishing, 1992.

Mack, Alison. *Dry All Night.* Boston: Little, Brown, 1990.

Martin, Katherine L. *Does My Child Have a Speech Problem?* Chicago: Chicago Review, 1997.

McNamara, Barry E., and Francine J. McNamara. *Keys to Parenting a Child with Attention Deficit Disorder.* Hauppauge, N.Y.: Barron's Educational Series, 1993.

Mrazek, David, and William Garrison. *A to Z Guide to Your Child's Behavior.* New York: Putnam, 1993.

Nosek, Kathleen. *The Dyslexic Scholar: Helping Your Child Succeed in the School System.* Dallas: Taylor, 1995.

Pueschel, Siegfried M., James C. Bernier, and Leslie E. Weidenman. *The Special Child: A Source Book for Parents.* Baltimore: Paul H. Brooks, 1988.

Robertson, Mary M., and Simon Baron-Cohen. *Tourette Syndrome: The Facts.* New York: Oxford University Press, 1998.

Shimberg, Elaine Fantle. *Living with Tourette Syndrome.* New York: Simon and Schuster, 1995.

Weiss, Lynn. *Attention Deficit Disorder in Adults.* Dallas: Taylor, 1992.

APPENDIX

GLOSSARY

Antidepressant: a medication that works to chemically prevent feelings of depression.

Apnea: a pause in normal breathing.

Attention-deficit/hyperactivity disorder (ADHD): a condition characterized by a consistent pattern of inattention and of activity and impulsivity.

Behavior modification: a technique that uses reinforcement to encourage desirable behaviors and discourage undesirable behaviors.

Chromosome: a strand of matter in the nucleus of a cell that contains the individual's genetic information.

Dyslexia: reading disorder.

Electroencephalogram (EEG): a recording, taken by a machine, that traces brain waves.

Encopresis: incontinence of feces.

Enuresis: incontinence of urine.

Fine motor coordination: control of the small muscles in the hands. Lack of fine motor coordination makes writing, artwork, and other detailed handwork difficult.

Gross motor skills: coordination of the large muscles in the arms, legs, and body. An individual who lacks gross motor skills typically appears clumsy and awkward and has difficulty with athletics.

Hypertension: high blood pressure.

Learning disorder: a condition characterized by achievement on individually administered, standardized tests in reading, mathematics, or written expression that is substantially below achievement expected for age, schooling, and level of intelligence.

Mental retardation: significant subaverage intellectual functioning and significant limitations in various adaptive skills, with onset before age 18.

Obsessive-compulsive disorder: a psychological condition characterized by recurrent obsessions (persistent thoughts or ideas) or compulsions (repetitive, ritualistic behaviors) that are time-consuming or distressing and that significantly impair a person's life.

Pervasive developmental disorder: a condition characterized by severe and pervasive impairment in several areas of development, including social interaction and communication skills.

Phenylketonuria: an inherited metabolic disease that can result in mental retardation. Children with this condition cannot metabolize the amino acid phenylalanine.

Placenta previa: a medical crisis that occurs during pregnancy when the baby's placenta becomes detached from the uterine wall. This condition can cause the baby to be deprived of oxygen and can be life threatening to both the baby and the mother.

Psychosocial intervention: treatment of a psychological disorder that addresses the emotions of the individual as well as his or her family or other social environment.

Psychostimulant: a medication that affects a person's emotional state by stimulating increased neurochemical functioning.

Syndrome: a group of symptoms that tend to occur together in a recurring pattern.

Tic disorder: a condition characterized by muscular or vocal tics (brief involuntary behaviors that serve no purpose) that are repeated over and over.

Toxemia: an abnormal condition during pregnancy in which the kidneys fail to work efficiently, allowing toxic substances to accumulate in the blood. Toxemia endangers both the baby's and mother's well-being.

APPENDIX

PICTURE CREDITS

page

8: © Shirley Zeiberg

10: Michael Escoffery, *Circle of Love* (1996). © Copyright ARS, N.Y., private collection.

12: © Hanna Schreiber/Photo Researchers

13: © Shirley Zeiberg

18: AP/Wide World Photos

20: John P. Kelly/The Image Bank, 1995

22: © David M. Grossman/Photo Researchers

28: Steve Dunwell/The Image Bank, 1994

30: National Library of Medicine

31: © Johannes Hofmann/ Okapia/Photo Researchers

34: © Shirley Zeiberg

37: © Shirley Zeiberg

39: Library of Congress, Washington, D.C.

41: © Spencer Grant/Photo Researchers

44: Photofest. © 1988 United Artists Pictures, Inc. All rights reserved.

47: © Shirley Zeiberg

48: Steve Murez/The Image Bank, 1998

51: © Bettmann/Corbis

54: © Ellen B. Senisi/Photo Researchers

56: © Shirley Zeiberg

62: AP/Wide World Photos

63: © Ellen B. Senisi/Photo Researchers

64: AP/Wide World Photos

67: © CLEO Photography/Photo Researchers

70: AP/Wide World Photos

72: Tomek Sikora/The Image Bank, 1996

74: © Richard Hutchings/Photo Researchers

75: B. Busco/The Image Bank, 1996

80: Ross Whitaker/The Image Bank, 1998

82: © Shirley Zeiberg

83: © Owen Franken/Corbis

Senior Consulting Editor Carol C. Nadelson, M.D., is president and chief executive officer of the American Psychiatric Press, Inc., staff physician at Cambridge Hospital, and Clinical Professor of Psychiatry at Harvard Medical School. In addition to her work with the American Psychiatric Association, which she served as vice president in 1981–83 and president in 1985–86, Dr. Nadelson has been actively involved in other major psychiatric organizations, including the Group for the Advancement of Psychiatry, the American College of Psychiatrists, the Association for Academic Psychiatry, the American Association of Directors of Psychiatric Residency Training Programs, the American Psychosomatic Society, and the American College of Mental Health Administrators. In addition, she has been a consultant to the Psychiatric Education Branch of the National Institute of Mental Health and has served on the editorial boards of several journals. Doctor Nadelson has received many awards, including the Gold Medal Award for significant and ongoing contributions in the field of psychiatry, the Elizabeth Blackwell Award for contributions to the causes of women in medicine, and the Distinguished Service Award from the American College of Psychiatrists for outstanding achievements and leadership in the field of psychiatry.

Consulting Editor Claire E. Reinburg, M.A., is editorial director of the American Psychiatric Press, Inc., which publishes about 60 new books and six journals a year. She is a graduate of Georgetown University in Washington, D.C., where she earned bachelor of arts and master of arts degrees in English. She is a member of the Council of Biology Editors, the Women's National Book Association, the Society for Scholarly Publishing, and Washington Book Publishers.

Daniel Partner is an author who lives and works in northern Vermont. His recent books include *The One Year Book of Poetry* and *Women of Sacred Song: Meditations on Hymns by Women.*